D

HISTORY OF ENGLISH

10 FEB

73211

IN THE SAME SERIES

Editor: Richard Hudson

HISTORY OF ENGLISH

Jonathan Culpeper

London and New York

First published 1997
by Routledge
11 New Fetter Lane, London EC4P 4EE

Simultaneously published in the USA and Canada
by Routledge
29 West 35th Street, New York, NY 10001

Typeset in Times Ten and Univers by
Florencetype, Stoodleigh, Tiverton, Devon

Printed and bound in Great Britain by
Redwood Books, Trowbridge, Wiltshire

British Library Cataloguing in Publication Data
A catalogue record for this book is available from the British
Library

Library of Congress Cataloguing in Publication Data
A catalogue record for this book has been requested

ISBN 0–415–14591–0 (pbk)

CONTENTS

USING THIS BOOK

Unlike traditional textbooks, this book aims to involve readers as much as possible in conducting their own investigations. You will find a series of numbered exercises in each unit, especially towards the end. These exercises are important: they are not 'add-on extras'. They will exemplify *and* move beyond the points made in the commentary. In addition, during the commentary, you may find short tasks in square brackets. It is worth noting that many of these exercises and tasks could be expanded to form extensive projects.

A number of the exercises will ask you to consult a dictionary. To do these exercises, you will need access to a dictionary which contains historical information, such as how a word was created and how its meaning might have changed. Probably, the best dictionary for the purpose is the *Oxford English Dictionary* (2nd edn, 1989) (hereafter, the *OED*). This is available in many libraries. However, reading an entry from the *OED* can be rather daunting. To help you do this, you will find that Appendix I describes some key features of *OED* entries. If you have not got access to the *OED*, don't panic! There is a whole series of dictionaries which are derived from the *OED* (e.g. the *Compact OED*, the *Shorter OED*, the *Concise OED*) and most of these will prove sufficient. Alternatively, you could try a specialist etymological dictionary, such as the *Oxford Dictionary of Etymology* (edited by C.T. Onions, Oxford: Clarendon Press, 1966) or Eric Partridge's *Origins: a Short Etymological Dictionary of Modern English* (London: Routledge, 1966), though the range of words covered is not as great as in the *OED*.

What if you get stuck on one of the exercises? Many skeletal 'answers' are in Appendix IV, but this appendix does not include 'answers' for exercises which can be worked out by using a reference work (e.g. a dictionary), which involve you working on your own data, or which ask you about your own language usage.

A particular feature of this book is the 'mini-corpus' of texts contained in Appendix III. During the course of this book, you will often be referred to specific texts. The texts have been selected to illustrate changes that have occurred in English over time. In some cases, they also present the views of commentators on the language. You could of course expand the range of texts. But a word of caution: beware of modern editions in which the language has been modernised or 'cleaned up'. In particular, editors have been fond of changing the original punctuation. An excellent source of texts is Dennis Freeborn's *From Old English to Standard English* (London: Macmillan, 1992). This book contains numerous facsimiles and painstakingly accurate transcriptions.

At the end of every unit, you will find a number of follow-up readings for the topic of that particular unit. Frequently, you will be referred to the relevant pages in David Crystal's *Encyclopedia of the English Language* (Cambridge: Cambridge University Press, 1995). This is comprehensive, clearly written and will become widely available. For more general reading, Appendix V offers some suggestions.

ACKNOWLEDGEMENTS

In writing this book, I have run up an overdraft of debts. My thanks go to Julia Hall, for suggesting I write the book; to Gerry Knowles for inviting me to join him in developing the first-year undergraduate course from which this book arises, for commenting on some parts of the book and for acting as an on-call consultant; to Jonathan Hope for casting a 'historical eye' over the book; to an army of students for commenting on the manuscript; to Jean Warnes for giving the perspective of an 'A' level English Language teacher; to Greg Myers for helping me to eradicate any potential problems for a US readership; to Dick Hudson for his efficiency and astute remarks; to Louisa Semlyen and Miranda Filbee for their support; and to Elena Semino for more than I can say.

Sources for Appendix III
Text 1: from a facsimile of the *Peterborough Chronicle*, in Dennis Freeborn's *From Old English to Standard English* (London: Macmillan, 1992). Text 2: from *A Middle English Reader*, edited by O.F. Emerson (London: Macmillan, 1905). Text 3: from *The Prologues and Epilogues of William Caxton*, edited by W.J.B Crotch (Oxford: Oxford University Press, 1928). Text 4: from a facsimile of the Public Record Office document SCI 59/5, in *The Cely Letters: 1472–1488*, edited by A. Hanham (Early English Text Society, London: Oxford University Press, 1975). Text 5: from *The Complete Works of Shakespeare*, edited by Peter Alexander (London and Glasgow: Collins, 1951). Text 6: from *The Authorised Version of the English Bible 1611*, edited by W.A. Wright (Cambridge: Cambridge University Press, 1909). Text 7: from a facsimile of the *Areopagitica* (Henston: Scholar Press, 1968). Text 8: from a facsimile of *A Short Introduction to English Grammar* (Henston: Scholar Press, 1967). Text 9(c): from Mark Sebba's *London Jamaican: Language Systems in Interaction* (London: Longman, 1993: 14).

Other sources
The examples in Exercise 4.4 are quoted from Keith Waterhouse's *English our English* (Harmondsworth: Penguin, 1991). The information for Table 8.1 is taken from T. Pyles and J. Algeo *The Origins and Development of the English Language* (Fort Worth, TX: Harcourt Brace Jovanovich, 1993: 110).

Permissions
Text 9 (a) is cited by kind permission of IMCO Group Ltd; Text 9 (b) by permission of Cow & Gate Nutricia; the Tango slogan by permission of Britvic Soft Drinks Ltd; and the extract in Appendix I, which is taken from *The Oxford English Dictionary* (2nd edn, 1989), by permission of Oxford University Press.

Trademarks
Sellotape is a trademark of Sellotape GB Ltd. Scotch is a trademark of the 3M Company.

THE BIRTH OF ENGLISH: CLUES IN PLACENAMES

1

> The most important factor in the development of English has been the arrival of successive waves of invaders and settlers speaking different languages. The history of placenames in Britain is closely connected to the dominance of various languages at various points in time.

English does not originate in Britain. Long before the Germanic tribes that became the English people arrived, Britain was inhabited by various Celtic tribes, of which the Britons were one. The history of the Celtic tribes stretches back more than a couple of thousand years. However, the impact of the Celtic languages on English has been rather minimal. In fact, the predominant legacy is in place-names. The placenames below all have some distant Celtic link:

Cities: Belfast, Cardiff, Dublin, Glasgow, London, York

Rivers: Avon, Clyde, Dee, Don, Forth, Severn, Thames, Usk

Regions: Argyll, Cumbria, Devon, Dyfed, Glamorgan, Kent, Lothian

EXERCISE ✎

1.1 Consider the list of placenames above. What areas of the British Isles seem to be well represented? Can you guess why this might be?

We cannot be sure what these placenames might have originally meant. Like many other placenames, they pre-date written records, which are preserved in significant quantities only from about

AD 700. Indeed, the study of the history of placenames in general is characterised by guesswork. With Celtic placenames we can compare words in surviving Celtic languages, such as Welsh, or consider the geography of the places in question. Thus, we can be fairly certain about the meaning of the following Celtic placename elements:

Pen (Welsh *pen*) = top, hill (e.g. *Pen*dle)

Lin (Welsh *llyn*) = pool (e.g. *Lin*coln)

Etymology

To study the history of words, whether placenames or any other type of word, is to study their ETYMOLOGY. Etymology will be an important issue in both **Units 4 and 5**.

The first invaders of Britain were the Romans, who arrived in AD 43 and occupied much of Britain for roughly the next 400 years. The Romans often Latinised existing Celtic placenames, rather than inventing completely new names. *London* is a Celtic placename supposedly based on the personal name *Londinos*, meaning 'the bold one'. The Romans seem to have simply made this more like Latin by changing it to *Londinium*. Few placenames surviving today are straightforwardly based on single Latin words. One example is *Catterick*, which is derived from Latin *cataracta* (= a waterfall). Nevertheless, there are a few important Latin placename elements, notably:

castra = a camp, walled town (e.g. Lan*caster*)

portus = port (e.g. *Ports*mouth)

via strata = paved way, a 'street' in a town (e.g. *Strat*ford)

The English language has its roots in the language of the second wave of invaders: the Germanic dialects of the tribes of north-western Europe who invaded Britain in the fifth century, after the Romans had withdrawn. According to the Venerable Bede (a monk at Jarrow writing in the eighth century), the year AD 449 saw the arrival of three tribes – Angle, Saxon and Jutish. Map 1.1 shows where these tribes are thought to have come from (there is particular uncertainty about the location of the Jutes).

Collectively, these Germanic settlers are usually referred to as the Anglo-Saxons, but from the very beginning writers of these Anglo-Saxon tribes referred to their language as *Englisc* (derived from the name of the Angles). This and subsequent invasions account for some of the current diversity in the languages and dialects of Britain. We shall look at the history of the various English dialects more closely in **Unit 10**. What happened to the native Celtic-speaking tribes of Britain? There was certainly no dramatic conquest by the Anglo-Saxons, but a rather slow movement from the east of Britain to the west, taking place over some 250 years. Where the Anglo-Saxons settled there is evidence of some integration with the local population. However, the Anglo-Saxons never got as far as the northern and western extremes of Britain. The Celtic languages –

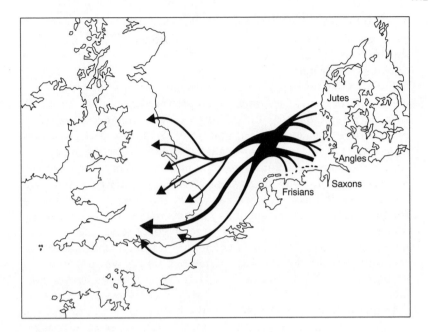

MAP 1.1   Angle, Saxon and Jutish Invasions

notably Cornish, Welsh and Scottish Gaelic – proceeded relatively independently of English in what are today Scotland, Wales and Cornwall. Each established its own literary tradition, and, excepting Cornish, which died out in the eighteenth century, are living languages today.

Thousands of English placenames were coined by the Anglo-Saxons in this early period. Common placename elements include:

burh = fort (e.g. Canter*bury*)

dun = hill (e.g. Swin*don*)

feld = open land (e.g. Maccles*field*)

ford = river crossing (e.g. Ox*ford*)

tun = farm, village (later developing into 'town') (e.g. E*ton*)

ing = place of (e.g. Claver*ing*)

ingas = followers of (e.g. Hast*ings*, Read*ing*)

ham = settlement, homestead (e.g. Nort*ham*)

hamm = enclosure, land in a river bend (e.g. Chippen*ham*)

The final four elements give rise to potential difficulties in deciding the meaning of Anglo-Saxon placenames, since the modern place-name spelling may not distinguish the original elements. In distinguishing *ham* and *hamm*, sometimes the only solution is to check the local landscape, in particular to see whether a river is present.

This problem of spelling disguising the roots of words is in fact a more general problem in the study of placenames, and, indeed, in the study of words in general. We always need to be cautious in drawing conclusions.

Let's consider how placename elements combine to form place-names. *Swindon*, for example, is created by combining the words *swine* (= pigs) and *dun* (= hill). This process of joining words to form **Compounding** other words is called COMPOUNDING. We will look at this process in more detail in **Unit 5**. Note that by investigating placenames we can learn about the culture and economy of the time. *Swindon* is a hill where, presumably, pig farming used to take place. A dominant trend in Anglo-Saxon placenames is that they take on the name of the tribal leader. For example, the first elements of the placenames *Macclesfield*, *Hastings* and *Chippenham* come from the personal male names *Mæccel*, *Hæsta* and *Cippa*. This trend highlights the fact that Anglo-Saxon society was patriarchal: power was concentrated in the hands of the leader, who, judging by placenames, was usually male.

In the ninth century, Britain saw the beginning of a third wave of invaders – the Scandinavian Vikings. Arriving from Denmark, Norway and Sweden, they soon took over the east of England and were only halted when King Ælfred, the king of Wessex in the south-west, won a decisive victory over the Danish King Guthrum in 878. The following year a treaty was drawn up whereby the Danes retreated to the east of a line running roughly from Chester to London, an area which became known as Danelaw (see Map 1.2).

The significance of this boundary is that it had the effect of increasing dialectal differences between the north and the south. These differences between north and south are still apparent today, and we will consider them further in **Unit 10**. One can also see the effect this boundary had on placenames. Words derived from Scandinavian languages (Old Norse and Old Danish) frequently appear in northern and north-eastern placenames – the shaded areas in Map 1.2. Common placename elements include:

by = village (e.g. Kirk*by* or Kir*by*, Cros*by*)

thorp = village (e.g. Miln*thorpe*)

thwaite = glade, clearing (e.g. Hawthorn*thwaite*)

Aspects of Scandinavian society are sometimes reflected in place-names. The following placenames all contain words indicating a particular rank in Scandinavian society.

Holderness = *hold*'s or yeoman's headland

Dringhoe = *dreng*'s or free tenant's mound

Lazonby (Lazenby) = *leysingi*'s or freedman's village

As with Anglo-Saxon placenames, a number of Scandinavian place-names were formed by adding the name of the tribal leader (e.g.

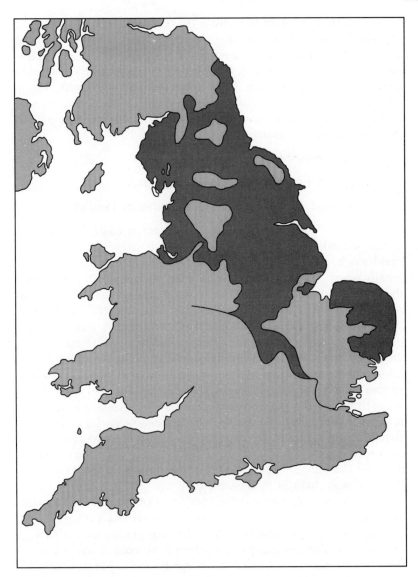

MAP 1.2 The Danelaw (from David Graddol, Dick Leith and Joan Swann, *English: History, Diversity and Change* (London: Routledge/Open University, 1996), p. 109)

Corby = Kori's village; *Formby* = Forni's village). In some cases, an Anglo-Saxon tribal leader's name was simply replaced by a Scandinavian one. Sometimes this led to a situation where within one placename there was a word of Scandinavian origin as well as one of Anglo-Saxon origin. The classic example is *Grimston*, which combines the Scandinavian personal name *Grímr* with the Anglo-Saxon word *tun* (= village). Such words of mixed origin are called HYBRID FORMS.

Hybrid forms

The fourth wave of invaders were the Norman French who arrived in 1066. Norman French became a prestige language spoken by the upper classes and used for administration. Most traditional place-names were left unchanged, perhaps so that administration could continue smoothly, but there were some exceptions. As with Anglo-Saxon and Scandinavian placenames, sometimes the personal name of the local lord of the manor or powerful family became part of the placename. For example:

Melton *Mowbray* (Roger de Moubray)

Leighton *Buzzard* (the Busard family)

Stanstead *Mountfitchet* (the Montifiquet family)

However, note that French personal names often stand alone, usually as the second word in a placename. This is suggestive of the fact that French, unlike the other languages we have considered, did not greatly interfere with the basic traditional placename. In some cases, the pronunciation of the traditional placename was slightly changed so that it would be easier for a French speaker to say. For example, Nottingham originally had the (perhaps less attractive from the point of view of today!) name *Snotingeham*. The first two sounds are an unusual combination for a French speaker, so the [s] was dropped. [*Stop*! You have just encountered a symbol designed to represent a speech sound. Turn to Appendix II and read the short explanation there.] Possibly the most common French words to be incorporated into placenames are *beau* and *bel* which mean beautiful or fine (e.g. *Beaulieu* = beautiful place; *Beaumont* = beautiful mountain; *Belvoir* = beautiful view). These positive terms were sometimes used to improve the image suggested by a placename, as when *Fulanpettæ* 'foul pit' was changed to *Beaumont*.

What about more recent developments in placenames? In Britain, very few new placenames have been coined. According to one source, about 98 per cent of current English placenames originated before 1500. The few placenames which have been recently created tend to commemorate famous events and people. For example:

Battles: Waterloo, Maida Vale, Peacehaven

People: Nelson, Telford, Peterlee

An interesting modern development is the transference of a place-name from one country to another. For example, *Waterloo* is trans-ferred from the name of a place near Brussels where the famous battle took place in 1815. However, for plentiful examples of place-name transference it is best to look outside Britain and in particular at areas of the world which were subjected to British colonisation. In the United States, for example, we find the transferred British placenames *Birmingham, Bristol, Cambridge, Canterbury, Lancaster, New Castle, Norwich, Swansea,* and many others. However, it is not the case that British colonisers could operate in total isolation from the local population. In many cases local placenames survived, despite the colonisers' attempts to create a second England by transferring placenames out of Britain. As a result, in former British colonies one typically finds a mixture of transferred British placenames and native placenames. To a certain extent, the same is true of the English spoken by the colonisers: it came into contact with the local language and adopted some of its particular characteristics, leading to a distinct variety of English. This globalisation of English is an important development and we shall return to it in **Unit 12**.

EXERCISES ✎

1.2 If you live in Britain, investigate the placenames of your area. If you do not live in Britain, use a fairly detailed map of Britain and select a particular area. Take at least fifteen placenames and use the readings suggested at the end of this unit to discover how those placenames came about. Classify your placenames according to (a) the period in which they were devised; (b) etymology, i.e. Celtic, Latin, Anglo-Saxon, Scandinavian, French; (c) the kind of element involved (e.g. personal name, description of local landscape or vegetation, commemorative); and (d) the form of the placename (e.g. a single word, a compound, a hybrid). Try to relate any trends you discover to historical or cultural factors.

1.3 English spelling, for reasons which we will consider in **Unit 3**, is not a reliable guide to pronunciation. In order to talk about pronunciation, we need to have some way of representing speech sounds on paper, and a possible system for transcribing sounds is introduced in Appendix II. Some placenames provide dramatic examples of the gulf between pronunciation and spelling. Here are some examples of placenames and a transcription of their pronunciations:

Leominster	[lemstə]	Lympne	[lɪm]
Causewell	[kæsl]	Meopham	[mepəm]
Quernmore	[kwɔːmə]	Farthingstone	[færəkstən]
Letheringsett	[lɑːnset]	Leycourt	[legət]

Can you work out how these placenames should be pronounced without consulting Appendix II? Check with a friend to see whether you can agree on the pronunciation of those which you are not sure about. Are there placename pronunciations in your region which seem fairly distant from the spelling? If so, try to write down a transcription of the pronunciation.

1.4 To what extent did British colonisers use transferred British placenames?

(a) Investigate the placenames of Australia. You could just consider the most important placenames in Australia, or, with a more detailed map, the placenames of a particular state.

(b) Investigate the placenames of the United States. You could make the study more interesting by comparing three states: one from the east, one from the south and one from the west. Make sure that you sample the same number of placenames from each state.

You will need to devise your own classification system, perhaps including such categories as transferred placenames (with subcategories according to where the placename was transferred from, e.g. Britain, France), biographic (with subcategories according to the nationality of the person the place was named after), language derivation (with subcategories according to the language involved, e.g. English, French, Spanish, Aboriginal, Indian). At the conclusion of your investigation, calculate percentages for your various categories, so that you can compare the relative importance of different types of placename.

DISCUSSION POINT

Just as placenames can be revealing, so can personal names. The earliest hereditary surnames appear shortly after the Norman Conquest. Investigate the history of your surname. Does your name seem to be associated with a particular language? Is it associated with a particular region? Is it in fact originally a placename? Is it the name of an occupation, or does it specify a particular family relationship?

If you are part of a group, find out the histories of other surnames. Are there particular trends within your group?

SUMMARY

■ In its earlier history, Britain has been populated by a number of different peoples (Celts, Romans, Anglo-Saxons, Scandinavians, French) speaking different languages. This diversity has had an important effect – as we shall see during the course of this book – on the way the English language has developed.

■ By investigating the etymology of placenames, we can appreciate the influence of a diverse range of languages at various points in time, and also gain insight into the social, cultural and economic history of Britain.

The key pages on placenames in David Crystal's *Encyclopedia of the English Language* (Cambridge: Cambridge University Press, 1995) are pp. 140–7. For a discussion of personal names see pp. 148–53. The best introductory book on the topic of placenames is Kenneth Cameron's *English Place-Names* (London: Batsford, 1961). Most public libraries stock books on local placenames, usually in the reference section. E. Ekwall's *The Concise Oxford Dictionary of English Place-Names* (Oxford: Clarendon Press, 1960) is a valuable source of information. For American placenames a good source of information is George R. Stewart's *A Concise Dictionary of American Place-Names* (New York: Oxford University Press, 1970). A good introductory book on surnames is P.H. Reaney's *The Origin of English Surnames* (London: Routledge, 1967). For reference purposes, the best work is P. Hanks and F. Hodges' *A Dictionary of Surnames* (Oxford: Oxford University Press, 1988).

FOLLOW-UP READING

2 INVESTIGATING CHANGE IN ENGLISH

> English is constantly changing, and all parts of the language have been affected. These changes have occurred for a variety of reasons.

Imagine that you have stomach ache and you go to the doctor. The doctor would ask you to describe your symptoms – you groan, clutch your stomach – and also to describe the relevant background to your symptoms. You would probably be asked such questions as: When did the trouble start? Have you eaten anything that might have caused it? Has it affected your appetite ... your bowels? By investigating the medical history relevant to your present state, the doctor can learn more about your stomach ache. I say relevant because obviously a doctor would not ask you such a question as: Has your big toe been hurting? Now, the case with language is similar. By investigating the history which is relevant to the present state of the English language, we can gain insight into that language, we can begin to explain how it got to be as it is. For example, we can explain why it is that we have such apparently crazy spelling: how it is that words come into existence; why it is that sometimes we seem to have a choice of words to express more or less the same thing (e.g. *fortunate* and *lucky*); where the confusing apostrophe–*s* (e.g. *student's* or *students'*) came from; why it is that we don't all talk like the queen or the people on the BBC; and so on. By looking at how English has changed, and the factors that have influenced those changes, we can begin to answer questions like these.

The fact that English has changed is plain to see. Look at Text 1 in Appendix III, written in the ninth century. It looks alien, and it is difficult to read without special training. Compare this with Text 2, written by a contemporary of Chaucer in 1387. It is usually possible to get the gist of Chaucer without the aid of a dictionary.

Shakespeare, as in Text 5, seems to be much more familiar waters, although it is not all plain sailing. When we reach the eighteenth century, exemplified in Text 8, our problems seem reduced to the occasional word. And finally with the twentieth century, we may feel that we have reached home ground. However, just because the English language becomes more comprehensible as it nears our present day, it doesn't in any way mean that the language has stopped changing. Consider a couple of recent changes: the word *euro-sceptic* has been formed to refer to someone opposed to any kind of European union; the word *grunge* can now be used to refer to a type of popular music. The general point I'm making is that all living languages are in a state of change.

The texts I referred to above fall within different periods in the development of the English language, and, traditionally, scholars have defined and labelled these periods in particular ways. Text 1 falls within the period known as Old English (OE), running from about AD 450 to 1100. Text 2 is written in Middle English (ME), approximately spanning the years 1100–1500. It may come as a surprise to some of you to learn that Text 5, the Shakespeare, is usually considered part of Modern English (Mod.E), which runs from 1500 to the present day. However, Modern English is often sub-divided: Early Modern English (EMod.E) spans the years 1500 to about 1750, and Late Modern English (LMod.E) spans the remaining years. Of course, these are conventional labels for these periods: there is no hard-and-fast rule that says, for example, Middle English finishes in 1500 and Modern English begins. In fact, you will find that different scholars often put the boundaries in slightly different places. Certainly, it is not the case that somebody apparently speaking Middle English in 1499 suddenly started speaking Modern English in 1501. This scenario would imply that the language didn't change within these periods, but then underwent a cataclysmic change when it reached a boundary. This is not the case: language is in a continual state of change. Nevertheless, whilst some caution is needed, these terms are convenient labels for these periods, which, very broadly speaking, correlate with major linguistic changes as well as major cultural, social and political changes. Consider, for example, these historical events. Old English is often dated from the arrival of Anglo-Saxon settlers in 449. The Norman Conquest in 1066 is obviously important in defining the beginning of Middle English. William Caxton's introduction of the printing press in about 1476 is an important factor in suggesting the beginning of Modern English: printing promoted a national standard for written English, as we shall see in **Unit 11**. Of course, these periods are characterised by more factors than this. You will discover more about the linguistic changes that took place during these periods in the following units.

What has changed in the English language? It is possible to find changes at every level of language.

EXERCISE

2.1   Have a close look at Text 1 in Appendix III. My word-for-word translation does not reflect what we would naturally do in contemporary English; it sounds awkward. So, write a fluent, easy-to-read version (in particular, this will require changing the order of words, adding words and changing the punctuation).

Now, look back through all the different versions and consider how they have changed. (This is rather like a spot-the-difference competition.) Note down as many of the linguistic changes as you can, using the grid below. In the left-hand column of the grid you will find that language has been broken down into different levels. More technical names for these levels are given in parentheses. To the right of this column I have suggested a series of questions you can ask yourself – questions which should help you to decide what features of Text 1 to place under a particular linguistic level. The right-hand column is for your examples (of course, you can always expand this on a separate piece of paper). You will experience difficulty with one linguistic level – 'Sound'. Clearly, you cannot hear Text 1. I suggest you leave this level blank for now. I shall discuss 'Sound' and 'Writing', and some examples from Text 1, in the following unit. The main aim of this task is that you should gain some experience in identifying linguistic features at different levels. Don't worry if you cannot find a comprehensive list of features for every level from Text 1. In the following units we will be focusing on each of these linguistic levels and on many more example texts.

Linguistic Level	Questions to ask yourself	Examples from Text 1
Writing (Graphology)	Are unfamiliar letters, spellings and punctuation marks used? What words are capitalised?	
Sound (Phonology)	How are words pronounced? Are there unfamiliar speech sounds?	
Structure (Grammar)	Are there unfamiliar endings on words? In your contemporary version have you had to supply extra words not present in the original? Have words been placed in an unfamiliar order?	
Words (Lexis)	Are there unfamiliar words?	
Meaning (Semantics)	Are there words used with unfamiliar meanings?	

A note of caution needs to be sounded about comparing two different texts written at two different points in time. We need to make sure that we compare like with like, or, if this is not possible, we need to be aware of any potential distortion in our observations. Comparing, for example, a religious text with a speech would be hazardous, since religious texts, and to a lesser extent poetry and legal texts, often contain archaisms, whereas spoken language often contains novelties. Thus, a comparison of Text 5 (which is literary and, more importantly, purports to be spoken dialogue) with, say, Text 1 (which is a rather formal written historical record) would need to be conducted with some caution.

Why does the English language change? Here are some possible reasons:

(a) Some changes within the language have come about largely as a result of the fact that language operates as a system – change in one part can cause change in another part, in effect a chain reaction. To take a simple example, during the Renaissance, scholars, influenced by Latin, decided to add *h* to a number of words. Thus, although in Middle English the word for 'throne' was spelt *trone*, scholars added an *h*, because the Latin word was spelt *thronus*. This resulted in the first sound of the word being pronounced differently, [θ] instead of [t]. A similar change occurred in the words *thesis*, *theatre*, *anthem* and *Katherine*. So, a change in graphology – a change in spelling – led to a change in pronunciation.

(b) Think of a situation where two languages are spoken within the same country or community. The languages are brought into close contact, some members of the community will speak more than one language and frequently switch between languages. This language or 'code switching' will lead to the mutual influence of those languages. This is an important factor when you bear in mind the invasions and settlement of Britain by peoples – such as the Scandinavians and French – speaking diverse languages.

(c) When considering the effect of other languages on English, speakers' attitudes need to be taken into consideration. French was and still is a high-prestige language for the English, as were the classical languages, Greek and Latin. Thus people copied these languages for social reasons, perhaps to sound more sophisticated or cultivated. The reverse is also true. For example, for the Germans, French has not been a high-prestige language, and as a result has had little effect on German, despite the fact that Germany is adjacent to France.

(d) The changes that have occurred in our physical environment, our culture, our social structures, our social attitudes and so on are often reflected in the language, particularly in vocabulary and meaning. Consider the following examples of new words and (in parentheses) the developments they reflect: *euro-sceptic* (political), *politically correct* (social attitudes), *user friendly* (technological), and many words for Italian cooking, such as *pesto*, *balsamic* vinegar, *fusilli* (cultural).

EXERCISES ✎

2.2   What strikes you as new and fashionable in the language today? Write down as many examples as you can. Now consider to what linguistic level these innovations belong. Do this before reading on.

Various factors influence people's perceptions of what is new. One factor relates to the fact that change occurs faster and more dramatically at some linguistic levels than others. Typically, change at the levels of phonology (sound) and grammar (structure) takes place rather slowly, whereas change at the level of lexis (words) is much faster.

2.3   Write down as many new words as you can (perhaps using some of the examples from the above exercise), and ask other people for suggestions. Use a dictionary to check that they really are new (say, not more than fifteen years old). Now, analyse your words and try to classify them into groups, according to the developments they reflect. What do your results tell you about external changes?

2.4   Where would you put the stress in the words below – on the first syllable or the second?

applicable, comparable, controversy, lamentable

Test these words on a group of young people, and then compare your results with a group of much older people. If you have discovered trends amongst the two groups and those trends differ, can you now identify a general shift in the stress of polysyllabic words like these? Of course, one can only guess that such a change will be completed: a language change can always fizzle out or even be reversed.

DISCUSSION POINT

One influence on language change has been the rules or ideas devised by people in authority. Language can reflect attitudes about language, because people often try to do what they think they should be doing. For example, my junior-school teacher told me never to begin a sentence with the word *and*, and, as a consequence, I tend not to. In fact, it only takes a quick look through the *OED* entry on *and* to realise that beginning a sentence with *and* is a useful way of conveying a number of particular meanings, and that it has a well-established history. Now, write down some of the rules or ideas that influence your language usage. If you are part of a group, gather up people's lists, and draw up a list of the most frequently mentioned rules. In this way, you should gain some insight into what the most popular 'dos' and 'don'ts' are. Now discuss the following questions: Are all linguistic levels covered? Do people really follow all these rules? Do the rules apply equally, and are they followed equally in speech and writing? If not, what does this suggest about differences in change in speech and writing? Is any rationale given for these rules?

SUMMARY

- English, in common with all living languages, is in a continual state of change.
- Change occurs at all levels of the language.
- Change can take place at varying speeds, or even be reversed.
- Change in one part of the language system can lead to changes in other parts of the system.
- Change is likely to occur when languages are mixed.
- Speakers are likely to imitate prestige languages.
- Language change can reflect changes in the physical environment, culture, social structure, social attitudes, etc.

FOLLOW-UP READING

Chapter 2 of Dennis Freeborn's *Varieties of English* (2nd edn, London: Macmillan, 1993) provides an overview of the development of English and an analysis of a text. For books discussing linguistic change in general, try Jean Aitchison's *Language Change: Progress or Decay?* (2nd edn, Cambridge: Cambridge University Press, 1991) or R.L. Trask's *Language Change* (London: Routledge, 1994).

3 SPELLINGS AND SPEECH SOUNDS

> English spelling used to represent speech sounds in a relatively simple way, but a variety of changes have led to a much more complex system.

Does spelling represent the pronunciation of words? Let's compare English spelling with Italian. The word for *enough* in Italian is *basta*. The letters of *basta* represent the sounds of the spoken word (pronounced like *pasta*, except for the opening sound). Generally when these sounds occur in other words they are represented by the same letters. Now consider *enough*. Clearly, the spelling does not represent the units of sound that make up the spoken word in a straightforward way. When these sounds occur in other words, they can be represented by other letters. In each of the pairs below, the italicised letters represent the same sound:

enough announce
enough much
enough fat

Phonemic

Unlike Italian, English spelling is not always PHONEMIC. There is no simple one-to-one correspondence between phonemes – the smallest units of speech distinguishing one word from another – and the letters that represent them. However, this is not quite so true of spelling in the Old English period. For example, consider the words *twa* ('two') and *lang* ('long') given in Text 1. The *w* of *twa* was originally pronounced, and thus, unlike today, each letter of the spelling corresponded to a phoneme of the spoken word. Similarly, the final *g* of *lang* was pronounced, so that the pronunciation of the word would be [laŋg]. Indeed, the final *g* of this word and of others (e.g. *tongue*, *ring*) is still pronounced in some west central areas of England.

So, generally, Old English spelling did not contain 'silent letters'. Why has the spelling system become less phonemic? Why is it now so complicated? History, as we shall see, can provide an explanation.

EXERCISE ✎

3.1 Given that spelling used to represent much more closely the pronunciation of words, what can you infer about changes in the pronunciation of the following words? (*Hint*: consider the letters that do not correspond to any of the sounds in your own pronunciation of these words.)

two, sword, answer

walk, half, folk

wreck, write, wring

gnat, gnarl, gnaw

knee, know, knight

The first problem was that English adopted the Roman alphabet, in other words, the alphabet of another language – Latin. Today we have over forty phonemes in English, but only twenty-six letters by which to represent those phonemes. In particular, note that we have about twenty vowel sounds in English, but only five vowel letters. Even in Old English the Latin alphabet on its own was not enough. In addition to Latin consonant letters, the Runic 'thorn' þ and the Irish Gaelic 'eth' ð were used, fairly interchangeably, for the phonemes [ð] and [θ] that we now represent with *th*. Some Old English phonemes were represented by pairs of letters, which we call DIGRAPHS. For example, *sc* was used to represent the first phoneme [ʃ] in the Old English word *scep* 'sheep', and *cg* was used for the last phoneme [ʤ] in the Old English word *ecg* 'edge'. In addition to Latin vowel letters, the letter 'ash' æ was developed by combining *a* and *e*, and was used for the phoneme [æ] that we now represent with *a*. Also, the digraphs *ea* and *eo* were used, as in the Old English words *eare* 'ear' and *beor* 'beer'. (Examples of some of these letters can be found in Text 1.)

Digraphs

EXERCISE ✎

3.2 It should be remembered that in Old English and Middle English there were no firm conventions for spelling. Greater variation was tolerated than would be today. In particular, a writer's spelling would tend to reflect whatever dialect they happened to speak. (We will consider this further in **Unit 10**.) The *OED* attempts to list the variant spellings of words. To get an idea of the degree of spelling variation, check the spellings of the following words: *spear*, *sword* and *shield*.

A number of the apparent oddities of English spelling were introduced by Middle English scribes, particularly Norman scribes who adapted spelling to suit French spelling conventions. Digraphs promoted by Middle English scribes include:

- *sh* replacing *sc* in words like OE *scip* 'ship'.
- *qu* replacing *cw* in words like OE *cwen* 'queen'. (Note that *cw* was in fact a much more obvious representation of the first phonemes of words like *queen*.)
- *gh* replacing *h* in words like OE *riht* 'right'.
- *ch* replacing *c* in words like OE *cin* 'chin'.
- *wh* replacing *hw* in words like OE *hwæt* 'what'.
- *c* replacing *s* in words like OE *is* 'ice'. (Consider the pronunciation of *c* in French words such as *Citroën*.)
- *ou* replacing *u* in words such as OE *wund* 'wound'. (Consider the pronunciation of *ou* in French words such as *vous*.)

Some of these innovations were actually advantageous. Until the adoption of *ch*, *c* had represented two phonemes: the first sounds of the words *chin* (OE *cin*) and *king* (OE *cyning*). Thus, *ch* helped make a useful distinction. The adoption of *ou* helped to indicate a long vowel without having to use double *u*. The problem with double *u* was legibility. The characters *u*, *uu*, *i*, *n*, and *m* were all written with straight down-strokes and were thus in danger of being confused. In fact, to make things clearer, scribes sometimes wrote *o* for *u* and *y* for *i*. Thus, the word *love* was once spelt *luve*, a spelling that was closer to pronunciation but not so legible.

Standardisation

The advent of printing with William Caxton in 1476 was a step towards the STANDARDISATION of spellings. Printing was most economic if one set of spelling conventions reflecting one dialect was chosen. We shall consider the choice of dialect Caxton made in **Unit 11**. For now, let's note that printing made possible the production of a vast amount of reading material using one set of spelling conventions: it could promote a 'standard' in spelling. This is not to suggest that the early printers entirely agreed on what the standard should be or were consistent in applying it. In some respects the printers added to the oddities of spelling. Many of the early printers were Dutch. Sometimes Dutch spellings influenced English words. For example, the word *ghost* in Old English was spelt *gast*, but the Dutch printers added an *h*, presumably influenced by the Flemish word *gheest*. Furthermore, the Dutch printers used continental characters. Thus non-Latin letters, such as 'thorn' þ, were not well represented. In fact, a *y* was chosen to represent 'thorn'. A remnant of this can be seen in the sign *Ye Olde Tea Shoppe*, where *Ye* is equivalent to *The*. This sign also illustrates other characteristics of Early Modern English spelling, which printers were at least partly responsible for.

Printers often added a superfluous *e* (e.g. *Olde*), doubled up consonants (e.g. *Shoppe*), or used *y* instead of *i* because they took up more space. This was done in order to increase the length of a line so that it would match the others of a text. All this added to the general variability in spelling. Line justification today, as in this very text, is automatically achieved on a word processor without varying the spelling.

EXERCISE ✎

3.3 Study the spelling in Texts 3 and 6. What inconsistencies in the spelling can you find? Can you explain why some of these occur? Consider the use of the letters *v* and *u*. At this time a *v* could be used for a *u* and vice versa, but they were not completely interchangeable. What determines the use of one letter or the other? The letters *i* and *y* are sometimes said to be interchangeable. How true is this of Text 3?

In the sixteenth century, there was particular interest in the classical languages Latin and Greek, and these had much prestige. It was fashionable to respell words in order to make them look more like the originals, although this meant adding 'silent letters'. These ETYMOLOGICAL RESPELLINGS include:

Etymological respellings

ME *langage*	>	*language* (Latin *lingua*)
ME *dette*	>	*debt* (Latin *debitum*)
ME *receite*	>	*receipt* (Latin *receptum*)
ME *samon*	>	*salmon* (Latin *salmo*)

However, sometimes the respellers got their etymology wrong. For example, it was assumed that ME *iland* came from French *isle*, and thus an *s* was added to make *island*. In fact, *iland* was an Old English word, and has Germanic roots. [Consult Texts 2 and 3 for the old spelling of *language*.]

In the sixteenth and seventeenth centuries, many words entered English from languages such as French (e.g. *grotesque, colonel*), Latin (e.g. *necessary, relaxation*), Greek (e.g. *chaos, pneumonia*), Italian (e.g. *piazza, piano*) and Spanish (e.g. *canoe, tobacco*). The important consequence is that English spelling contains the spelling conventions of other languages: it is an amalgam of various spelling systems. This process of borrowing from other languages has continued throughout the development of English. More recently, the spelling of the word *khaki* – the colour – reflects the fact that it is borrowed from Urdu, and the spelling of *kamikaze* reflects the fact that it is borrowed from Japanese.

Many people in the sixteenth century were highly critical of the tremendous variation in spelling, the addition of superfluous letters and so on. Also, from this time onwards dictionaries started to appear which people could consult for an authoritative spelling.

Coupled with printing, all this had the effect of fixing or standardising spellings. In fact, very few spellings have changed since Dr Johnson's dictionary of 1755. [Check the spelling in Text 8, written in 1762. How does it differ from today's?] Unfortunately, spellings were fixed at a time of great confusion. Not only was there a great influx of words from other languages, but the language was also experiencing changes in pronunciation – changes which spelling failed to keep up with. We have already seen in Exercise 3.1 how certain consonants ceased to be pronounced. Even more dramatic changes occurred in the pronunciation of long vowels, the so-called **Great Vowel Shift**. GREAT VOWEL SHIFT. These changes can account for why the relationship between spelling and pronunciation in words like *make*, *sweet* and *ride* is not as simple as it once was. We'll consider the Great Vowel Shift further in **Unit 10**, and here just illustrate the general nature of the changes with one example. The vowel of *sweet* used to be pronounced like the vowel of the word *set* except that it was longer, as indeed the double *e* suggests. Practise this pronunciation and compare it with today's. Think about where in your mouth you make the two vowels. It should appear to be the case that today's vowel is articulated higher up and further towards the front of the mouth. During the Great Vowel Shift vowels articulated at the front of the mouth were raised and fronted, and vowels articulated at the back were raised and backed.

Changes since the eighteenth century have mainly been to do with attitudes towards the spelling system that emerged. The old tolerance of spelling variation evaporated, and spelling came to be seen as an indicator of education and even intelligence. This century a number of attempts have been made to simplify spelling, the most famous campaigner for spelling reform being George Bernard Shaw. However, spelling reform has so far failed to produce any changes in British English spelling. In American English, spelling reform – promoted in particular by Noah Webster – has achieved a measure of success, leading to such spellings as *color* and *center*.

EXERCISES ✎

3.4   In this unit we have primarily considered spelling in terms of whether there is a correspondence between phonemes – the units of speech – and the letters of words. In fact, the relationship between spelling and spoken words may be systematic, but more complex than simple one-to-one correspondence of phonemes and letters. Let's take an example. How would you pronounce the word *ghoti*? Most of us, I guess, would pronounce it as 'goaty'. Bernard Shaw coined this word to illustrate the apparent absurdities of spelling. He claimed that it should be pronounced like *fish*: *gh* as in *enough*, *o* as in *women*, and *ti* as in *nation*. But clearly spelling does not work like this; 'goaty' is the more obvious pronunciation of *ghoti*. Shaw fails to take into account the more complex ways in which spelling indicates pronunciation, such as by the position of letters in a word.

Construct an attack on Shaw's claim. What evidence can you give to support the claim that *ghoti* should be pronounced 'goaty'and not like *fish*? (*Hint:* think of other words that begin or end with the same letters.)

3.5

(a) Many of the final -*es* on words are remnants of old grammatical endings, and were pronounced as a 'schwa' (a short vowel sound, as in the first phoneme of the word *about*). Towards the end of the Middle English period these final -*es* ceased to be pronounced. However, whilst they no longer corresponded in a simple way with single phonemes, many did provide useful information about the pronunciation of a word. Consider the words *fate*, *bite* and *mope*, with and without the final -*es*. What pronunciation information does the final -*e* convey? Can you find examples where this generalisation doesn't work?

(b) In Old English a doubled consonant would affect the pronunciation of that consonant, as is the case in Italian. Today this is no longer the case: *t* would be pronounced the same as *tt*. However, doubling a consonant does provide pronunciation information. Consider the following pairs of words: *sitter/seater*, *shutter/shooter*, *chatting/charting*, *wedding/wading*. What pronunciation information does the doubled consonant convey? Can you find examples where this generalisation doesn't work?

3.6 In one particular study, the following were found to be common misspellings: *gallary*, *succesful*, *exhibition*, *definate*, *politition*, *extasy*, *morgage*. (1) On the basis of these misspellings, describe some potential problems in English spelling. (2) Discover why these words have troublesome spellings. (*Hint:* trace the origins of these words.)

Imagine you are asked to reform the spelling system. What changes would you make? Would you change the whole system or only part of it? What difficulties might you encounter in making your changes?

DISCUSSION POINT

If you are part of a group, you may wish to create a debate on spelling reform. Divide the group into two. One half should argue in support of spelling reform, and the other against it, defending spelling as it is now.

SUMMARY

- Spelling has become less phonemic over the years.
- A basic problem is that there are not enough letters to represent phonemes on a one-to-one basis.
- A number of oddities in spelling were introduced by Middle English scribes, particularly the Normans, and later by the early printers.
- Etymological respellings have added to the number of 'silent letters'.
- English spelling is complicated by the fact that it contains the spelling conventions of other languages.
- Beginning in the fifteenth century, a standard spelling system had fully evolved by the eighteenth century. But spellings were fixed when great changes were occurring in pronunciation.
- Much social prestige is now attached to conforming with the standard.

FOLLOW-UP READING

The key pages on English spelling in David Crystal's *Encyclopedia of the English Language* (Cambridge: Cambridge University Press, 1995) are pp. 272–7. Also, check out the discussion of letters and sounds for Old English (pp. 16–19), Middle English (pp. 40–3) and Early Modern English (pp. 66–7 and 69). Probably the best available historical discussion of English spelling is D.C. Scragg *A History of English Spelling* (Manchester: Manchester University Press, 1974). An interesting overview appears in Chapter 7 of Francis Katamba *English Words* (London: Routledge, 1994).

BORROWING WORDS

4

One of the most dramatic changes in the English language has been the expansion of vocabulary. In particular, this has been achieved by importing words from other languages.

The extract below is from the BBC comedy series *Yes Prime Minister*, whose principal characters are the government minister James Hacker and the civil servant Sir Humphrey. In his diary, Hacker recalls the time when Humphrey told him that he was going to move to another department:

> Humphrey had said that 'the relationship, which I might tentatively venture to aver has not been without a degree of reciprocal utility and even perhaps occasional gratification, is approaching the point of irreversible bifurcation and, to put it briefly, is in the propinquity of its ultimate regrettable termination'.
>
> I asked him if he would be so kind as to summarise what he's just said in words of one syllable.
>
> He nodded in sad acquiescence. 'I'm on my way out', he explained.
>
> (J. Lynn and A. Jay, *The Complete Yes Prime Minister*, (London: BBC, 1989) p. 16)

Sir Humphrey uses a mysterious bureaucratic language to disguise the indiscretions of government and defuse any moments of potential embarrassment. Hacker is a relatively straightforward person who needs things to be put in simple language. It is almost as if they speak two different languages.

EXERCISE ✎

4.1 Do Hacker and Humphrey speak words that come from different languages? Compare Humphrey's words quoted in the first paragraph with his words quoted in the final paragraph. Use a dictionary to find out which languages these words are derived from.

There is a contrast between the loftiness of Sir Humphrey's first utterance and the mundane tone conveyed by the vocabulary of his final speech. This, as you will have discovered, can be explained by noticing that the two sets of words differ in their origin: the majority of the first set comes from Latin or French; the second set is part of the Anglo-Saxon word stock of Old English, and as such it is Germanic. In the course of this unit you will find out about the different sources of our vocabulary, and about the different associations words of different origin have acquired.

Let's begin a brief history of English borrowing by noting that even before the Angles, Saxons and Jutes had arrived in England bringing their Germanic dialects that gave rise to English, they had borrowed some Latin vocabulary. However, as far as we know, this amounted to only a few dozen words (e.g. *wall*, *street*, *cheap*, *wine*), and thus Old English vocabulary was overwhelmingly Germanic.

Loanwords

Thus, it contained very few LOANWORDS, contrasting with the situation in Middle English and Modern English, where loans proliferate. One estimate is that 3 per cent of Old English vocabulary consisted of loanwords, whereas 70 per cent of today's English consists of loanwords. This difference is of great importance in explaining how the English language has changed over time.

Many Germanic Anglo-Saxon words have survived into Modern English with very little change in either form or meaning (e.g. *god*, *gold*, *hand*, *land*, *under*, *winter*, *word*). The majority of the few loanwords in Old English were from Latin. This is no great surprise, given the fact that religious texts were written in Latin and the early Christian missionaries were influential in spreading literacy. They introduced some 450 Latin words into the language, mainly to do with the Church (e.g. *altar*, *angel*, *cleric*, *nun*, *temple*, *psalm*, *city*, *master*, *demon*).

The Scandinavian Vikings invaded and settled in England from the ninth to the eleventh centuries. Anglo-Saxon English and the Scandinavian languages (Old Norse and Old Danish) were all Germanic languages, and to some extent mutually comprehensible. This close similarity made it easy to adopt words into all areas of vocabulary (e.g. *are*, *die*, *leg*, *want*, *get*, *both*, *give*, *same*, *they*, *them*, *their*), not just words with specialised content, such as religious vocabulary. About 1,800 words of Scandinavian origin have survived into present day English, including very common words. The word *are*, for example, became part of the verb *to be* – the most common verb in English. [Note the use of *are* in the word-for-word translation of Text 1, where it replaces the Old English word *sind*.]

After the Norman invasion of 1066, French became the official language of law and administration. The ruling classes spoke French, and popularised French dress, cooking and etiquette. Even when English displaced French after about 200 years, French culture exerted a powerful influence. Over 10,000 words were adopted from French during the Middle English period (e.g. *parliament*, *baron*, *manor*, *noble*, *liberty*, *government*, *arrest*, *judge*, *jury*, *prison*, *beef*, *lettuce*, *mutton*, *pork*, *sausage*, *dress*, *jewel*, *cloak*, *virtue*, *art*, *beauty*, *romance*). In many cases Old English words were replaced by French ones (e.g. OE *stow* – Fr. *place*, OE *wyrd* – Fr. *fortune*). Where both survived, meanings would drift apart. Consider the pairs OE *house* – Fr. *mansion*, OE *bloody* – Fr. *sanguine*.

An enormous number of the French borrowings had originally come from Latin. There were also several thousand direct Latin borrowings into English, particularly towards the end of the Middle English period. Most of these were from areas such as religion, science, law and literature (e.g. *scripture*, *client*, *conviction*, *library*, *scribe*, *dissolve*, *quadrant*, *medicine*, *ulcer*). However, it was not until the Renaissance in the sixteenth century that borrowing from Latin took off. The Renaissance saw the development of new concepts and techniques, the flowering of the arts and sciences, as well as further exploration of the world. Much of this took place on the continent of Europe. Learning was given a boost by printing, and books became widely available. However, many literary, scientific and religious texts were in Latin, since Latin was the language of scholarship and scholarly literature. To make these texts more widely available, people began to translate them into English, often using a Latin word in the translation when no good English equivalent could be found. The upshot of these developments was that words from many languages were adopted into English, but especially words from Latin and the Romance languages French, Italian and Spanish. Around 13,000 new loanwords entered the language in the sixteenth century alone, and of these some 7,000 were from Latin. Examples of Latin loanwords include *absurdity*, *benefit*, *exist*, *exaggerate*, *external*, *obstruction*, *relaxation*, *relevant*, *vacuum*, *virus*, *excursion*, *fact*, *impersonal*, *expectation*, *exact* and *eradicate*.

More recently, there seems to be a general decline in borrowing from Classical and Romance languages. French borrowing has been in decline since the Middle English period, and Latin since the end of the seventeenth century. Why is this? One possible reason is that these languages experienced a decline in prestige: towards the end of the Middle English period, the upper classes ceased to speak French, and English became the language of administration; towards the end of the seventeenth century, English took over from Latin as the language of scholarship. Another reason is that English has gone global: it comes into contact with languages right round the world. As a consequence, English is now borrowing from languages which have not been traditional sources for vocabulary. For example, one study suggests that Japanese accounts for 8 per cent of borrowings in the last fifty years, and African languages for 6 per cent. A further reason is that although borrowing used to be an important source for new words, it is now of relatively minor importance, accounting for around 4 per cent of new words. Nowadays most new words are formed from the resources we already have, by compounding words, for example. We will consider such word creation in the next unit.

Today, it is clear that Germanic, French or Latin vocabulary has acquired a distinctive flavour of its own, and is used in different contexts and for different purposes.

EXERCISE

4.2

    (a) What impression do the extracts in Text 9(a) and (b) give? Describe the vocabulary used (use a dictionary to trace the origins of the words). Why is this particular vocabulary used in these particular extracts?

    (b) Using a dictionary, compare the vocabulary of Text 3 with the vocabulary of Text 7. Why is this particular vocabulary used in these particular extracts?

The more common words of English, particularly the words of speech, tend to be Germanic in origin, whereas Latin words tend to be rare and appear more often in written language. Germanic words are more likely to be used in informal, private contexts, whereas Latin words are the words of formal, public occasions. Germanic words tend to be simple, often words of one syllable, whereas Latin words are usually polysyllabic. [For an illustration of this, check the vocabulary of the *Yes Prime Minister* extract.] Concrete things are often referred to by words of Germanic origin (e.g. *wood*, *earth*, *house*, *pot*, *pan*, *knife*, *fork*), whilst Latin words tend to refer to more abstract concepts. Germanic words often express some kind of attitude, whether negative or positive, whereas Latin words tend to be more neutral (for example, compare the pairs *whore – prostitute* and *cheap – inexpensive*). These stylistic differences are summarised in the chart below. In terms of these scales, French words tend to lie between Germanic and Latin vocabulary.

Germanic	⟷	*Latin*
frequent	⟷	rare
spoken	⟷	written
informal	⟷	formal
private	⟷	public
simple	⟷	complex
concrete	⟷	abstract
affective	⟷	neutral

An important issue is *why* these areas of vocabulary have acquired particular characteristics. This can be explained by looking at the historical development of English loanwords. The bulk of Latin vocabulary entered the language during the Renaissance, which was a period of lexical upheaval. The important point is that, unlike the earlier borrowing of French vocabulary into speech, Latin vocabulary was the language of the written medium, the language of books or the 'inkhorn'. Much of it was difficult to understand (and still is!), and was perceived as 'alien' by some. Not surprisingly, it is in the sixteenth century that the first dictionaries appeared, in order to help people cope with these 'hard words'. This state of affairs gave rise to the so-called INKHORN CONTROVERSY, a debate about the merits or otherwise of the acquisition of 'artificial', 'bookish' Latin vocabulary – the vocabulary coming from the inkhorn – in place of 'natural', 'common' Germanic vocabulary.

Inkhorn Controversy

Some strands of the Inkhorn Controversy are still current today. The quest for a pure Anglo-Saxon vocabulary has continued over the centuries. However, as we have seen, there never was a pure Anglo-Saxon vocabulary: Latin loanwords were part of English vocabulary even before English came to England. A more practical consideration – and one that will become clear in the following unit – is that Latin and Germanic vocabulary are so thoroughly mixed that they would be very difficult to separate.

EXERCISES ✎

4.3 Read through the list of words below and give a rating out of five for each word, according to how formal you think it is (0 = very informal, 5 = very formal). (*Hint:* Think about whether you have come across the word before, and, if so, how formal the context was (e.g. ordinary conversation, religious or legal texts).)

fire	=	fear	=
holy	=	ascend	=
trepidation	=	flame	=
rise	=	sacred	=
conflagration	=	terror	=
mount	=	consecrated	=

Now rearrange the words above to form four rows of synonyms (i.e. words of similar meaning). Organise your rows so that they are in columns according to language of origin (e.g. Germanic, French or Latin). (Use a dictionary to find this etymological information.)

	Germanic	*French*	*Latin*
1			
2			
3			
4			

How does etymology correlate with formality? If you can, check your ratings with someone else's.

4.4   Keith Waterhouse, a contemporary commentator on the English language, offers the advice below. What seems to be the underlying basis for his advice? (*Hint:* consider the origins of the words he focuses on.) Are these words synonymous, as he implies – can we simply use one for the other? Is his advice helpful?

- Prefer short, plain words to long, college-educated ones. *End*, not *terminate*.
- Use concrete words, not abstract ones. *Rain*, not *inclement weather*.
- Avoid abstract adjectives. *Penniless*, not *penurious*.
- Do not use foreign words if you can help it. *£20,000 a year*, not *£20,000 per annum*.

DISCUSSION POINT

Sometimes present-day debates about keeping English plain and simple sound rather similar to the Inkhorn Controversy. What are the positive or negative aspects of using Latin or Germanic vocabulary? Can the avoidance of Latin vocabulary be helpful? Or, does the avoidance of Latin vocabulary have some negative consequences? In what way does it depend on what you are trying to do with your language (give some examples)?

If you are part of a group, set up a debate: half argue for Germanic vocabulary and half for Latin vocabulary.

SUMMARY

- The dramatic expansion of English vocabulary has been achieved through loanwords, mostly from French and Latin but also from Greek, Italian and Spanish.
- In more recent times, English has borrowed from a more diverse range of languages, and, more generally, borrowing as a method of increasing vocabulary has become less important.
- English words of different origin have acquired different stylistic associations, and tend to be used in different contexts.
- People have particular attitudes to words of different origin.

FOLLOW-UP READING

The key pages in David Crystal's *Encyclopedia of the English Language* (Cambridge: Cambridge University Press, 1995) are pp. 8, 24–7, 60–1 and 124–7. Francis Katamba provides a very good overview of borrowing in *English Words* (London: Routledge, 1994) Chapter 10. Most of the standard history of the English language textbooks contain a relevant section (e.g. Chapter 12 in T. Pyles and J. Algeo's *The Origins and Development of the English Language* (Fort Worth, TX: Harcourt Brace Jovanovich, 1993)).

NEW WORDS FROM OLD

5

> One way of creating new vocabulary has been to use already existing words. Over time, this method has become increasingly important.

Where do new words come from? In the last unit we looked at words borrowed from other languages, and in this unit we are going to look at how new words have been created from old. However, you may be wondering about words that are completely original creations, words that have no roots. The fact of the matter is that these are few and far between. One estimate is that below half a per cent of new vocabulary over the last fifty years is original. *Googol* – the word for the number 1 followed by a hundred zeros – is an example. It was brought into the world by a nine-year-old boy when his father, a mathematician, asked him for a suitable name for the number. Some rootless words are supposed to have been created to represent sounds, they are echoic or ONOMATOPOEIC. *Cuckoo* is the classic example and there are many others (e.g. *bleep, honk, bang*). Rootless words tend to crop up in literary texts, particularly fantasy and science fiction, but they rarely move into common usage, exceptions perhaps being *hobbit* and *triffid*. The point is that the vast majority of words have some kind of etymology – they have roots.

   How are words formed from the resources that we already have? Below is a checklist that outlines some of the ways in which words are formed.

AFFIXATION – adding affixes to form another word.   Affixes are short elements which usually do not exist as words in their own right, but are tacked on to a root word in order to form another. Affixes that are placed at the beginning of a word are called PREFIXES (e.g.

Onomatopoeic

Affixation

Prefixes

29

Suffixes

undress, **de**compose, **mis**fortune, **re**call) and affixes placed at the end of a word are called SUFFIXES (e.g. *trouble**some**, harmon**ise**, sing**er**, sin**ful**). Old English was well stocked with affixes, some of which are still amongst the most commonly used in English (e.g. *happy, quick**ly**, black**ness**, fool**ish**, heart**less***). Some Old English affixes are no longer used or are falling out of use. For instance, the prefix *for-* and the suffix *-lock* were once relatively frequently used, but now are largely confined to the words *forgive, forgo, forbid, forbear, forlorn, forsake* and *forswear*, and *wedlock* and *warlock*. Other Old English affixes fell out of use, but then experienced a revival. This happened to both *-dom* and *-wise*, which reappeared in words like *stardom, officialdom, likewise* and *pricewise* – a revival that in both cases was led by American English. The major change in English affixes over time has been expansion due to the acquisition of affixes from other languages. Just as English borrowed words, it also borrowed affixes. Examples include *anti-, -ism* and *micro-* from Greek (e.g. ***anti**-climax, Commun**ism**, **micro**wave*), *-al, ex-, multi-, non-* and *re-* from Latin (e.g. *accident**al**, **ex**change, **multi**-racial, **non**-stop* and ***re**build*), and *-ette* and *-esque* from French (e.g. *kitchen**ette*** and *pictur**esque***).

EXERCISE ✎

5.1 More than one affix can be used to create a word. How many affixes are in the following word, and from which languages have they been borrowed?

antidisestablishmentarianism

(*Hint:* Remember that many dictionaries list affixes as well as words, so you can check that what you think is an affix really is an affix.) Affixes can bring about a change in meaning or a change in grammar (e.g. the addition of *-ness* to the word *happy* results in a change from adjective to noun). Beginning with the root word *establish*, add on affixes and each time describe what changes occur.

Back formation

BACK FORMATION – *subtracting elements (often affixes) to form another word.* For example, the word *editor* appeared before the word *edit*. With the subtraction of the affix *-or*, English gained the word *edit*, the verb describing what the editor did. Similarly, *burglar* came before the verb *burgle*. An interesting example of back formation is the word *pea*, which comes from *pease*. Originally, *pease* was both the singular and the plural. However, because it sounded as if it had a plural ending, people invented *pea* to talk about a single pea.

Compounding

COMPOUNDING – *combining words to form another word.* We met the process of compounding in **Unit 1**. There are, in fact, three forms of compound: there are open compounds (e.g. *new born*), hyphenated compounds (e.g. *new-born*) and solid compounds (e.g. *newborn*). These compounding conventions are rather arbitrary, and there are differences between British and American English (for example, American English tends to avoid hyphenated forms). But, generally, older and shorter compounds are more likely to be solid. The above example is more likely to be solid than the more recent compounds *new town* or *new wave*. In fact, some very old compounds are barely recognisable as such. The word *lord* is an example. It began life as the compound *hlaf-weard*, meaning 'loaf-keeper', but even in Old English it had contracted to *hlaford*.

EXERCISES ✎

5.2 Use a dictionary to discover the words involved in the following compounds:

> lady, gossip, daisy, nostril, sheriff, goodbye

5.3 How old is the open compound *acid rain*? Have a guess. Now go and use a dictionary to see whether you were right.

It is very difficult to guess accurately the age of new words. Sometimes apparently new words have been lurking for years at the edges of vocabulary – often as specialised vocabulary – and only later make their way into mainstream usage. Computer terminology, for example, seems fairly new. However, most of it was coined in the 1950s and 1960s, and only with the advent of the PC in the 1980s did it become mainstream vocabulary.

Blends

BLENDS – fusing elements of two other words. In a sense, this is an extreme form of compounding. Classic examples include *smoke + fog > smog*; *motor + hotel > motel*; *breakfast + lunch > brunch*. Such blending of words occurs at the time the word is formed, and thus it is distinguished from a word like *lord* where fusion occurs over time.

Functional conversion

FUNCTIONAL CONVERSION – using one part of speech as another. For example, consider the conversion of nouns into verbs, or, more specifically, body-part nouns that have been used as verbs: to *head* a department, to *eye* someone up, to *nose* into somebody's affairs, to *neck* with someone, to *shoulder* or *elbow* somebody aside, to *hand* in an assignment, to *finger* one's watch, to *leg* it, to *knee* someone in the . . . , and so on. Shakespeare added 'to *lip* a wanton wench', though this did not gain general currency. Not only can nouns be converted into verbs, but it seems that almost any part of speech can be used as another. The words *up* and *down* would seem to be fairly limited words, but they too can be converted into nouns, as in expressions like *I'm coping with the ups and downs of life.*

EXERCISE ✎

Eponyms

5.4 One kind of functional conversion is when personal names (proper nouns) are converted into other types of word. A surprising number of such words or EPONYMS have been created this way. Use a dictionary to find out which people gave their names to the following words: *lynch, dunce, boycott, sandwich, cardigan, wellingtons, pasteurise, sadism, atlas, jovial, venereal, tantalise.*

Clips

CLIPS – shortening a longer word (usually by removing syllables). Clips involve the creation of a new shortened form of a word, which, in most cases, supplants the original word. Thus, we talk about a *bus* rather than an *omnibus*. For some peculiar reason, the set of vocabulary related to underwear consists largely of clips: *vestment > vest, pantaloons > pants, knickerbockers > knickers, brassière > bra.* Interestingly, British and American English sometimes varies with regard to the extent of a clip. Compare *advert* and *ad*.

Acronyms

ACRONYMS – combining the initial letters of words or syllables. Some words are quite clearly acronyms, for example, *TV* (*television*), *TB* (*tuberculosis*), *VD* (*venereal disease*), and *DIY* (*do it yourself*). Other words are less transparently acronyms, for example, *radar* (**ra**dio **de**tecting **and** **r**anging) and *laser* (**l**ight **a**mplification by **s**timulated **e**mission of **r**adiation).

There are two important points to bear in mind about these ways in which words can be created. First, they can overlap. There are a number of affixes, for example, which can also function as independent words, and so sometimes it is not clear whether affixation or compounding is involved. There is an issue, for example, with the suffix *-able*. The suffix is actually a borrowing of the Latin suffix *-ibilis*, which in French and later in English was sometimes spelt *-able*. However, in form it is identical to the adjective *able* (e.g. *He is able to do it*), which comes via French from the Latin word *habilem*. Thus with relatively recent words ending *-able* (e.g. *analysable, killable*), it is not clear whether we have a case of affixation or compounding. Second, these ways of creating words are not equally productive in generating vocabulary. Consider these approximate figures for sources of new vocabulary over the last fifty years:

Compounding	36%
Affixation	27%
Functional conversion	17%
Shortening (back formations, clips, acronyms)	9%
Blending	6%

In fact, compounding used to be even more important in English. This is not surprising, given that compounding is popular in Germanic languages and that English used to be more Germanic in character. However, with the great influx of loanwords, the development of English, unlike that of Modern German, did not have to rely so much on internal resources. For example (to continue the underwear theme of this unit!), English adopted the word *bra* (*brassière*) from French; Modern German has the compound *büsten-halter* (literally, 'bust-holder').

What types of language contain many new word formations? Literary texts are often said to be a source. In particular, Shakespeare is credited with many coinages, though one can never be entirely sure whether he really invented them or whether he was simply the first person to record what was already in the language. For example, by adding the affix *-less*, he made an adjective out of the verb *to count* in the line 'One sweet kiss shall pay this *countless* debt.' A new coinage, such as this, which enters the general word stock is called a NEOLOGISM. However, many words are formed for the 'nonce': they are one-off coinages for the particular purpose in hand; they tend to have relatively limited circulation and are quickly forgotten. These are called NONCE-FORMATIONS. For instance, Shakespeare's line 'Would'st thou be window'd [i.e. placed in a window] in great Rome' contains the nonce-formation *window'd*; though we now can talk about *framing* somebody, we cannot talk about 'windowing' them. As with literary texts, the language of advertising often displays word formation creativity in an attempt to capture the reader's attention. Sometimes product names enter the language as general vocabulary items. Consider terms for adhesive tape: Scotch tape (common in the United States) and Sellotape (common in the United Kingdom) are both registered trademarks.

Neologisms

Nonce-formation

EXERCISE ✎

5.5 Slang is a prolific source of new word forms. Using slang is a way of demonstrating membership of a particular social group. A characteristic of slang is that it is up-to-date and fashionable, and to maintain this, new word forms have to be invented all the time. Find a magazine, such as a music magazine, aimed at young people. Select an article and look for new word forms. Try to categorise them according to the classification outlined above.

Throughout the centuries people have expressed negative attitudes to certain word forms. Today, one still finds people writing to news-papers or television stations with their objections. In particular, hybrid forms, such as *television* (Greek *tele* + Latin *vision*) or *official-dom* (Latin *official* + OE *dom*), have been criticised. Sometimes pre-judices are expressed against particular affixes. The verb-forming suffix *-ise* (or *-ize*) in words like *finalise*, *prioritise*, *routinise* often provokes outrage. From a linguistic point of view, there is nothing that makes these word forms better or worse than others. The issue is a social one. As we saw in **Unit 2**, people tend to be conservative and dislike change whatever it is. Over time people accept innova-tions. For example, the word *beefeater*, which is now very much part of the establishment, is in fact a hybrid form: French *beef* + Germanic *eater*.

EXERCISE ✎

5.6 I have selected ten words for each of the twentieth, seventeenth, fourteenth and eleventh centuries from the *OED*, paying little attention to how the words came to exist in English. Go through the lists below and label the words using the same categories as above (i.e. compounding, affixation, functional conversion, shortenings, blending and borrowing). For instances of borrowing, also note which was the direct donor language. Don't try and trace the etymology of the words right back. For example, *introspect* is a seventeenth-century borrowing from Latin, and, for the purposes of this exercise, you can label it as such. However, if one went further back, one would find that it originated in Latin through a process of affixation: *intro-* (meaning 'inside') plus *spicere* (meaning 'to look').

Twentieth century	Seventeenth century	Fourteenth century	Eleventh century
AIDS	antihypnotic	ability	afterward
backslash	brilliant	colony	climb
Rambo	homework	colourless	consul
camcorder	introspect	communication	coolness
upgradable	delinquence	handmaid	guilty
buyout	diagnosis	labour	marshmallow
mousse (verb)	enema	predicament	millstone
trueish	piano	pupil	shepherd
perestroyka	undercurrent	presently	shorten
spreadsheet	manufacture (verb)	sixpence	undergo

Look across the centuries to see how frequently words were created via a particular process. Bear in mind that the sample of words you have for each century is extremely small, so concentrate on the bigger differences. What changes have occurred? In the light of the commentary in this and the last unit, can you explain why these changes have occurred?

DISCUSSION POINT

Think of as many new word forms as you can. Now go and check them in a dictionary. Are they genuinely new or are they just, for example, colloquial forms that have been in the language for years?

If you are part of a group, set up a competition to think up the newest word forms.

SUMMARY

- Few English words are original creations; most are borrowed from other languages or formed from existing vocabulary.
- The most important processes of word formation in English are compounding, affixation and functional conversion.
- Compounding was the most important way of generating new vocabulary in Old English. In the history of English, compounding seems to decrease in importance when borrowing increases.
- English has significantly increased its stock of affixes by borrowing from other languages.
- Words are formed with no apparent regard as to where the original elements come from, resulting in hybrid forms. These, as well as other new forms, have been the subject of complaint.

FOLLOW-UP READING

The key pages in David Crystal's *Encyclopedia of the English Language* (Cambridge: Cambridge University Press, 1995) are pp. 128–9. Also, check out the relevant sections on pp. 22, 61 and 198. T. Pyles and J. Algeo give a good overview (Chapter 11) in *The Origins and Development of the English Language* (Fort Worth, TX: Harcourt Brace Jovanovich, 1993), though some of their claims about the existence of new word forms may seem a little strange to some readers, since they are writing from an American perspective. Francis Katamba's *English Words* (London: Routledge, 1994) is also worth trying (parts of Chapters 4 and 9). If you are interested in words created from names, have a look at C.L. Beeching's *Dictionary of Eponyms* (London: Library Association, 1989); if you are interested in new words, try browsing through the *Oxford Dictionary of New Words* (1991).

6 CHANGING MEANINGS

> Changes in the meanings of words – semantic change – can be amongst the most striking and accessible examples of language change. However, one needs to be aware that meanings are subtle and complex, and not simply captured within a dictionary-type definition.

If you want to find out what a word means, what do you do? Most people would look the word up in a dictionary. Dictionaries can indeed shed light on meanings and how they arose, but must be treated with caution, because word meaning is more than a compact definition of the type we see in dictionaries. Word meaning, one might say, is like an onion: it consists of many layers, and its taste will vary according to how people use it – whether in a curry sauce or a bolognaise sauce. Knowing the meaning of a word is knowing how it is used. As words become used in different ways and in different contexts, they acquire different associations and so the meaning changes.

EXERCISE ✎

6.1

(a) If we had to think of a list of features or criteria that defined both the words *woman* and *lady*, one might suggest that they include being human, female and adult. A definition based on these lines would be the DENOTATIVE MEANING of the two words. But there must be more to meaning than this, since we know that there is a difference between these two words – we know they can be used to mean different things. Consider these words placed in the context of the sentences below.

Denotative meaning

She's only thirteen, but she's a woman already

She's only thirteen, but she's a lady already

What differences in meaning – what different associations or CONNOTATIONS – do the words have?

Connotations

(b) The meaning of words can be influenced by the words with which they tend to co-occur. *Pretty* and *handsome* both mean 'good-looking', but may be distinguished by the range of nouns with which they are likely to co-occur. Which of them would you put with the nouns below?

____village   ____garden
____woman   ____inheritance
____colour   ____proportions
____contribution   ____flower

On the basis of your choices, try to describe the differences in meaning between the two words. You may well have hesitated over *woman*. Both *pretty* and *handsome* could be used here, but each suggests a different kind of attractiveness.

(c) Words can carry with them stylistic associations – associations with particular types of language. In what types of language would you expect to find the words in the following sets: *cast – throw – chuck, steed – horse – nag*?

One way in which dictionaries try to give us clues about usage is by providing quotations where the word is used. However, even the dictionaries that do contain quotations cannot, for practical reasons, contain every usage of a word. It becomes a matter of selection and interpretation by the editor, and inevitably dictionaries lag behind actual usage. Let's compare two dictionary entries for the word *darky* (or *darkie*):

A Negro. [Informal]
(*Thorndike English Dictionary*, 1948)

A darkie is a very offensive word for someone who has brown or black skin.
(*Cobuild English Language Dictionary*, 1995)

The difference between the definitions is vast. The *Thorndike* prioritises the denotative meaning 'A Negro'; the issue of usage is relegated to parentheses and limited to a remark on the degree of formality. In contrast, the *Cobuild* dictionary is centrally concerned with the context of usage, in particular, what effect the word is likely to have ('very offensive'). It is clear that as a description of the meaning of *darky* the *Thorndike* dictionary is hopelessly inadequate, and as a guide to a student of the English language it borders on criminal negligence. We can speculate on why it is deficient: is it the policy of the dictionary to concentrate on denotative meaning, or is it a reflection of racist attitudes of the editor or even of the society of forty years ago? For the purposes of this unit it serves as a warning not to think that a word's associative meaning, acquired according to how a word is used, is less important than its denotative meaning. In fact, sometimes the associative meaning of a word becomes the defining denotative meaning of a word. For example, *sinister*, a borrowing from Latin, originally meant 'left' or 'left hand'. But even in Latin it had associations of bad luck. By the seventeenth century these associations formed the denotative meaning of the word, the notion of 'leftness' having died out.

The main ways in which words may change meaning include:

Specialisation

SPECIALISATION – *narrowing of meaning.* For example, the word *meat* used to refer to any kind of food, but now refers specifically to flesh. [Check the meaning of *meat* in Text 3.] The word *deer* used to refer to any kind of beast, but now refers to a particular four-legged wild animal.

Generalisation

GENERALISATION – *widening of meaning.* For example, the word *clerk* started with the sense of 'a member of the clergy'. This was extended to include 'scholar' and then 'types of office worker', and in American English to include 'a shop/hotel worker'. Similarly, the word *business* originally meant 'a state of being active', but the meaning was extended over time to include 'occupation', 'a piece of work', 'a concern, matter, affair', 'dealings', 'trade' and 'a commercial enterprise'.

Amelioration

AMELIORATION – *elevation of meaning.* For example, the word *pretty* began with the negative sense of 'cunning, crafty', and the word *shrewd* began with the negative sense of 'depraved, wicked'.

Pejoration

PEJORATION – *degradation of meaning.* King James II (1685–8) upon seeing the new St Paul's cathedral described it as 'amusing, awful and artificial', by which he meant it was wonderful. *Amusing* had the sense of 'capturing one's attention'; *awful* of 'being impressive, majestic (literally, full of awe)'; and *artificial* of 'being skilful, displaying art'.

Transfer

TRANSFER *of meaning.* Sometimes the meaning of a word shifts, so that the word refers to a different – though often closely associated – set of things. For example, the list below charts the main shifts in the meaning of the word *bureau*:

twelfth century	coarse woollen cloth
thirteenth century	cloth covering tables or counters
fourteenth century	counting table
fifteenth/sixteenth century	writing table
seventeenth century	room containing the table
	people working in the room
	department
	agency

One specific way in which meaning can be transferred is through metaphor. A metaphor involves talking about something in terms of something else.

6.2 Spot the metaphor: look through the list below and tick the examples which you think contain a metaphor.

(a) My teacher is a wonderful person
(b) My teacher is an encyclopedia
(c) My teacher causes daily earthquakes in the classroom
(d) My teacher frightens me enormously
(e) My teacher never runs out of batteries (I wish I could find the off button)
(f) My teacher is definitely not good-looking
(g) My teacher talks in fast forward
(h) My teacher fills my days with light

6.3 Metaphors are often used in the language of science and technology. A relatively new metaphor is the one used in the software advertisement below:

> destroyed files, changed or corrupted data ... you can avoid this with one shot of Norton Anti Virus Vaccine ... NAV is ready and waiting for the next strain of virus to appear ... viruses sneak in undetected, but NAV spots them first

What's the main metaphor used in this area? Why do you think it is used? Do you know of any computer virus names that involve this metaphor?

When a metaphor is used frequently, it becomes conventional and we gradually stop perceiving it as a metaphor. Such metaphors are called dead metaphors. For instance, the word *candid* now means 'frank, open, not hiding one's thoughts', but in its earliest history in English it could mean 'white' – the sense of the Latin word *candidus* from which it is derived.

6.4 Using a dictionary, investigate the dead metaphors in *comprehend, dilapidated, dependent, petrified.*

Of course, the above list of ways in which words have changed meaning, though fairly comprehensive, is not complete. Also, remember that (1) some words can be classified along a number of different dimensions, and (2) sometimes words shift their meaning as part of a set of words. In fact, some of the most interesting changes in word meaning have taken place in whole sets of related words.

EXERCISE ✎

6.5 The development of terms used to refer to women is particularly interesting. Using a good dictionary or an etymological dictionary, investigate the meaning of the words below. In particular, consider whether it has always been the case that these words only refer to women, and whether they originally had a neutral or favourable meaning, but have experienced pejoration.

dragon, hag, harpy, hussy, minx, mistress, scold, shrew, witch

DISCUSSION POINT

Are there word meanings you have used – or you have seen or heard used – which have been criticised (perhaps by a parent or a teacher)? For example, some people object to the use of the word *aggravation* to mean 'trouble caused by aggressive behaviour or harassment'. Talk to some other people, in order to compile a list of 'pet hates'. Why do you think people object to these meanings? How do they justify their objections? Do they appeal to a particular authority? Do you agree with them?

If you are part of a group, divide the group into two. Get half the group to write down their understanding of the words *infer* and *disinterested*, and the other half to write down their understanding of the words *imply* and *uninterested*. Now compare results. Is there a general distinction between *infer* and *imply*, and *disinterested* and *uninterested*? If no distinction arises, use a dictionary to find out if a distinction was made in the past. Is it a useful distinction?

SUMMARY

- Dictionaries are an important resource in discovering the meanings of words, but a dictionary is not the ultimate authority: it is shaped by the attitudes, abilities and policies of the editor and the compilers.
- The meaning of a word is not simply a list of distinctive features, the denotative meaning, but includes the equally important associative meaning, acquired according to how a word is used.
- Some of the main ways in which meaning has shifted include specialisation, generalisation, amelioration, pejoration and transfer.

The key pages in David Crystal's *Encyclopedia of the English Language* (Cambridge: Cambridge University Press, 1995) are pp. 138–9, and pp. 170–1 are also relevant. Most textbooks on the history of the English language contain a section on meaning or semantic change. There are also more specialised books that deal with meaning changes within particular words (e.g. A. Room's *Dictionary of Changes in Meaning* (London: Routledge, 1986), or J. Copley's *Shift of Meaning* (Oxford: Oxford University Press, 1961)). If you're interested in the history of words referring to women, try Chapter 10 of G. Hughes' *Swearing: a Social History of Foul Language, Oaths and Profanity in English* (Oxford: Blackwell, 1991).

FOLLOW-UP READING

7 PUNCTUATION

Punctuation plays an important role in the way we interpret texts. Over time, it has changed with respect to both form (the marks used) and function (what those marks do).

Woman without her man is helpless

What do you make of the above sentence? Shockingly sexist? Well, what about this sentence:

Woman: without her, man is helpless

Well, it is still sexist, but this time it is sexist to men. Clearly, punctuation plays an important role in determining the way we interpret words.

EXERCISES

7.1 Ask somebody to jot down the three sentences below when you say them, but vary the order in which you say them. Can you say them in such a way – with the appropriate intonation – that your writer supplies the punctuation you want?

You're cold.

You're cold?

You're cold!

Punctuation can in part make up for the fact we can't hear writing. It can tell you, for example, whether something is a statement, a question or an exclamation.

7.2 The passage below appeared in an exam paper set for some poor hapless students in 1914. They were asked to supply punctuation, including capital letters where necessary. It's tricky stuff, but have a go.

> o king they cried there is no one so mighty as you do all things obey me he asked there is nothing that dares to disobey you o king they cried will the sea obey me he asked command it o king and it will obey said one sea cried canute i command you to come no further

In performing this task you will need to work out which words go with which. For example, it is clear that the words in 'they cried' or 'the sea' should not be separated by punctuation, and neither should the words in 'i command you to come no further'. The point is that interpreting a text partly involves decisions about the structure – about the grammatical units of that text – and, in normal circumstances, we use punctuation to help mark off those units. This task will also give you a sense of the wide range of punctuation forms we have available today, including speech marks, for example. The fact that punctuation is thought to be the stuff of exam papers is in itself significant. Punctuation, rather like spelling, is perceived to be a mechanism for judging people's literacy and even intelligence. It is small comfort for students to find out – as you will do in this unit – that the punctuation system is a set of social conventions which developed as a result of expediency, fashion and the say-so of those with power (e.g. printers, grammarians, the Church), rather than being a system based on linguistic merit.

So far, we have been looking at punctuation in two respects: function and form. Punctuation now has a wide range of forms at its disposal, which have three main functions: first, and most importantly, to indicate the grammatical boundaries of a text; second, to indicate aspects that might be conveyed by reading aloud, in other words, aspects of PROSODY (e.g. intonation, stress, pauses); and, third, **Prosody** as we shall see, to indicate how the senses of different parts of a text relate to each other. We can label these functions grammatical, prosodic and rhetorical.

Punctuation in Old English was very different from today.

EXERCISE ✎

7.3 Analyse the punctuation of Text 1. The general question to ask yourself is: How does the punctuation differ from today's? And more specifically: What forms of punctuation are used? What function(s) does the punctuation have?

The idea of writing in lines and of signalling sections of texts with a capital or some particular mark (rather like we signal paragraphs through line indentation), had been established by the time of the earliest Old English writings in the seventh century. But there was certainly no shared punctuation system. Various systems had been devised for ancient Greek and Latin texts, but they were sporadically and variously applied even then. InfactmanyGreekandLatin textswerewrittenwithoutpunctuationmarksandwithoutspacesbe tweenwords. However, there was pressure for change from two directions. Scribes had to cope with Latin as a foreign language and began to add spaces, in order to help with word recognition. More importantly, the Church was concerned about the possible misinterpretation of religious texts, and thus a number of systems were developed. A particular feature of biblical punctuation is its concern for prosody: punctuation was designed to assist reading aloud. Indeed, this is still a feature of many biblical texts today.

EXERCISE

7.4   Text 6 contains an extract from the Authorised Version of the Bible (1611). Practise reading it out, following the clues suggested in the punctuation. Compare this with attempts at reading the 1914 exam text above.

Between the twelfth and fourteenth centuries there existed a generally accepted stock of punctuation marks. The 'punctus' or point roughly corresponded to our full-stop (.), and was primarily used to mark a pause (sometimes the length of this depended on the height of the point in the line). The 'punctus elevatus' was later replaced by the colon (:); the 'punctus interrogativus' corresponded to our question mark (?); and the 'virgula', a slash (/), later developed into our comma (,). By the fifteenth century, the exclamation mark (!) and the semi-colon (;) had begun to be used. What function did these marks perform? Unlike today, the emphasis was on prosody, and, particularly from the fifteenth century onwards, on rhetoric. Caxton, for example, pays little regard to grammar. This emphasis is perhaps not surprising, given that many texts were designed to be read aloud. Writing and reading to oneself were very much minority activities. Of course, all this assumes that punctuation was used in the first place and that it followed any kind of principle: the Middle English period is characterised by variation, and punctuation is no exception. Some texts, often more informal texts, received hardly any punctuation. Even today how 'heavy' or 'light' punctuation is, can depend on the type of text. Legal texts, for instance, contain very light punctuation. In addition, writers were often rather idiosyncratic, or even arbitrary, in their punctuation. Caxton is less than consistent in the way he punctuates.

7.5 Analyse the punctuation of Text 3 written by Caxton. How does the punctuation differ from today's? What forms of punctuation are used? Are there any guiding principles?

7.6 Compare Caxton's punctuation in Text 3 with that in Text 4, a letter produced at a very similar time.

7.7 The influence of rhetoric on punctuation is easiest to see if one examines a great stylist, such as Milton. Analyse the punctuation of Text 7. You will find that Milton is not thinking in terms of units such as 'sentences', but of the sense relationships between different parts of his text. To help understand this, jot down all the conjunctions (e.g. *and*, *but*, *as*, *for*) that immediately follow punctuation marks together with the marks that they follow. Now group those conjunctions according to the kind of relationship they signal, that is to say, whether they are additive (e.g. *and*), contrastive (e.g. *but*), comparative (e.g. *as*) or causal (e.g. *for*).

From the mid-to-late seventeenth century there was a shift of emphasis to grammatical punctuation. Numerous grammar books began to be published, often containing a section on punctuation, and printing conventions became more regular. In fact, in the eighteenth century excessive punctuation – compared with today's practices – was fashionable. Sometimes nearly every clause or phrase was marked off. Nevertheless, by the end of the eighteenth century, the stock of punctuation marks and their usage was very similar to today's. [To check the truth of this, read Text 8, written in 1762. What differences are there?]

7.8 Today we use capitals to indicate the beginning of a new sentence, proper nouns or forms of address (e.g. Sir, Ms, Mr). Consider Texts 7 and 8 and work out the rationale for the use of capitals.

How much variation is there in current punctuation practices? If you have not already done so, discuss the various ways in which the passage in Exercise 7.2 might have been punctuated. Are there particular areas of disagreement?

Do you have a light punctuation style or heavy? If you are part of a group, compare punctuation styles. You can do this by getting everybody to write a short formal letter; say, a letter thanking some-body for sending you three different books. Make sure that the letter includes an address, the date, greetings and partings (e.g. *Dear X* and *Yours sincerely*); and that the body of the letter contains only one sentence, but also lists the three imaginary book titles. Do this now.

Compare results. Give each letter a punctuation heaviness rating, according to whether punctuation was used in or at the end of (1) the address, (2) the date, (3) the greeting, (4) the parting and (5) the list. (That is, does a comma appear before *and*? Compare *oranges, apples and pears* and *oranges, apples, and pears*).

SUMMARY

- Today we have a wide range of punctuation forms, which perform three functions: grammatical, prosodic and rhetorical.
- The development of punctuation was given a boost by scribes struggling with a foreign language – Latin – and by the Church's concern for both the possible misinterpretation and the reading aloud of religious texts.
- Although there was a fairly common stock of punctuation forms in Middle English, there was also much variation in the application of these forms.
- The emphasis in function of punctuation had been prosodic and rhetorical, but in the seventeenth century this switched to grammatical.
- Today's punctuation was largely in place by the end of the eighteenth century.

FOLLOW-UP READING

Many of the standard history of the English language textbooks do *not* include a section on punctuation. However, you can find highly relevant sections in David Crystal's *Encyclopedia of the English Language* (Cambridge: Cambridge University Press, 1995), pp. 278–83 and 68.

GRAMMAR I: NOUNS

8

> Over many centuries, English has undergone an important shift in the way it signals grammatical information. The legacy of the past is still apparent in irregular plurals (e.g. *mice, sheep*) and the apostrophe–*s* (e.g. *Jonathan's book*).

Since the eighteenth century, grammar has been mystified or made into a kind of mental assault course which, apparently, sorted out those who were sophisticated and cultivated from those who were not. In fact, we all have a highly developed, complex and sensitive knowledge of grammar. The hitch, of course, is that we are often not aware of the knowledge that we have, and also that we often don't have the words to express that knowledge. One aim of this unit is to help you begin to solve this problem. However, it is true to say that grammatical change is more difficult to observe than, say, change in speech sounds. If you listen to older people or an old film, it's usually the pronunciation which is striking, not the grammar. We are less conscious of grammatical change, which takes place relatively slowly.

One of the most important differences between Old English and today's English is that in Old English grammatical information was typically signalled by the INFLECTIONS or endings of words. Today, there is one main inflection for nouns: a final -*s* (or -*es*) to signal number. By and large, if a noun has no -*s*, it is singular; if it has an -*s*, it is plural.

Inflections

EXERCISE ✎

8.1 Words borrowed from other languages can cause problems when it comes to deciding on how to make them plural or singular, because they do not take the regular English -*s* inflection. Are the following words plural or singular to you: *data*, *criteria*, *index*, *focus*, *formula*? How do you go about signalling a change from one to the other, or do you use the same form for both singular and plural?

If you look at Table 8.1, you'll see that there are six Old English nouns listed: *hund* (= any dog, not just a hound), *deor* (= any animal, not just a deer), *cild* (= child), *oxa* (= ox), *fot* (= foot) and *lufu* (= love). Each noun carries a set of different inflections that make up a DECLENSION for that noun. I'm giving them to you here so that you can appreciate how complex the inflections of nouns used to be, and so that I can explain some of the features of English we use today.

Declension

Table 8.1 Old English noun inflections

Number	Case	Noun declensions					
Singular	Nominative	hund	deor	cild	oxa	fot	lufu
	Accusative	hund	deor	cild	oxan	fot	lufe
	Genitive	hundes	deores	cildes	oxan	fotes	lufe
	Dative	hunde	deore	cilde	oxan	fet	lufe
Plural	Nominative	hundas	deor	cildru	oxan	fet	lufa
	Accusative	hundas	deor	cildru	oxan	fet	lufa
	Genitive	hunda	deora	cildra	oxena	fota	lufa
	Dative	hundum	deorum	cildrum	oxum	fotum	lufum

As you can see, these nouns vary according to number and according to case. What, you may wonder, are cases? In Old English, nouns used to have inflections which indicated the function or relationship of words to other words in the sentence; that is to say, these nouns had case endings. There were four main cases – nominative, accusative, genitive and dative – each signalling a different function:

Case	Typical grammatical functions
nominative	the subject of the sentence (e.g. **Australia** beat *England*)
accusative	the direct object of a sentence (e.g. *Australia beat **England***)
genitive	the possessor or source (e.g. ***Jonathan's*** book)
dative	the indirect object or recipient (e.g. *I gave **the librarian** a book*)

An important point to note about today's English is that one can change grammatical functions simply by changing the word order. For example, by swapping the countries *England* and *Australia* I change what is the subject and what is the object. *Australia beat England* is not the same as *England beat Australia*. In Old English, case endings signalled the grammatical roles of nouns in sentences, so in theory whatever I did to the word order there would still be one reading of the sentence. Consider the following sentences.

(1) Se guma syhð þone huntan   (nominative – verb – accusative)

    The man sees the hunter   (subject – verb – object)

(2) Se hunta syhð þone guman   (nominative – verb – accusative)

    The hunter sees the man   (subject – verb – object)

(3) Se guma þone huntan syhð   (nominative – accusative – verb)

    The man the hunter sees   (?? – ?? – verb)

The nouns *guma* and *hunta* follow the same pattern as the noun *oxa* in Table 8.1. The nominative form has a final -*a*, and the accusative has a final -*an*. Thus, in sentence (1), clearly the man is the subject (i.e. he is doing the seeing) and the hunter the object (i.e. he is being seen). In sentence (2), who is doing what changes, and so the inflections change too. (Note also that the word 'the' changes its form according to case: *se*, if it is nominative, and *þone*, if it is accusative). The important sentence is sentence (3). Here, it is clear in the Old English version that it is the man (*guma*) who sees the hunter (*huntan*), but today's version – *the man the hunter sees* – could, in theory, be read both ways.

Today, we rely much more on word order to help us work out grammatical function. Usually the subject comes first, followed by the verb, and then the other parts of the sentence such as the object. This pattern was common in Old English as well, but word order was generally more flexible. Let's take an example from Text 1:

Erest weron bugend þises landes brittes
(first were inhabitants of this land Britons)
'The first inhabitants of this land were Britons'

Note that the verb 'were' occurs much earlier in the Old English sentence than in the present-day translation. Today we would generally put the whole of the subject – 'the first inhabitants of this land' – before the verb. This particular Old English example also illustrates the genitive case. Where today we would use the preposition *of* to indicate the relationship between the 'inhabitants' (*bugend*) and 'this land', in Old English they would use the genitive inflection -*es* (*þises landes*). Generally, prepositions such as *of* were used less in Old English. It might be noted at this point that this particular inflection – the -*es* – gave rise to the apostrophe–*s* which we use today. I shall return to this later.

EXERCISES ✎

8.2

    (a) In case you are feeling confused, bear in mind that personal pronouns are almost as complex now as they were in Old English, yet we use them without trouble. Like Old English nouns, they are marked for case. Underline the pronouns in the examples below according to whether they are nominative (the subject), accusative (the object) or genitive (the possessor).

1 He sees him
2 Him he sees
3 He sees his face

(b) Second-person pronouns used to be more marked for case and number than they are now. If you compare Table 8.2 for Middle English and Table 8.3 for today's English, you'll see that *you* has become the predominant form.

Table 8.2   Second-person pronouns in Middle English

Grammatical function	Singular	Plural
Subjective (nominative)	thou	ye
Objective (accusative)	thee	you
Possessive (genitive)	thy/thine	your/yours

Table 8.3   Second-person pronouns in today's English

Grammatical function	Singular	Plural
Subjective (nominative)	you	you
Objective (Accusative)	you	you
Possessive (genitive)	your/yours	your/yours

The Early Modern English period was one of transition with a mixture of *you* forms and *thou* forms. Interestingly, the factors that determined the usage of second-person pronouns in this period were not simply grammatical. The situation was somewhat like that in today's French (*tu* and *vous*) or German (*Sie* and *du*). *You* became a prestige form associated with the upper classes, whereas the opposite happened for *thou*. Speakers often exploited these associations: for example, *you* could be used to express politeness, whereas *thou* could be used to express condescension.

Look carefully at the usage of second-person pronouns in Texts 5(a) and (b) and 6. What is determining their usage? (*Hint:* Start by considering they simply follow the grammatical pattern given in Tables 8.2 and 8.3.) Can you explain why the second-person pronouns in Text 6 are governed by different principles?

What legacy did these noun inflections leave Modern English? To begin with, I shall be referring closely to the noun declensions in Table 8.1. Today's plural marker – the final -*s* – survives from the -*as* nominative/accusative plural form, as exemplified by *hundas*. In Old English there were other types of nouns with different plurals.

Over time the *-s* plural marker took control of most nouns. However, some of the other types of plural marking have survived and this has led to some variability today. *Deor*, to the right of *hundas*, has zero marking for plurality. This has survived today. It would sound awkward, if you spoke about 'deers'. *Sheep* also belongs to this noun declension, as did a lot of other nouns which have now been taken over by the *-s* plural.

Cild, the next declension, has an interesting plural. In Old English the plural was *cildru*. This form developed into *childer*. Have you heard the word *childer*? If you live in the north of England, it is possible that you have heard it. The *-n* of *children* was not present in Old English. *Children* acquired a second plural ending, the *-n* that is used in the noun declension to the right exemplified by *oxan*. *Brethren* has a similar history. The use of *-n* as plural ending used to be popular. In the Early Modern English period one often finds examples such as *eyen*, *shoen*, *housen*, *treen*, and the first two of these can still be heard in Scottish English. Now, in the majority of dialects, they all take the *-s* plural ending. The only pure survivor of this declension is *oxen*.

The following declension, exemplified by *fot*, is characterised by the fact that it not only had inflections but also changed the vowel of its basic form. Today, that vowel change *foot/feet* is a mark of the plural, but in Old English note that it is also found in the dative singular and that not all plural forms had it. Only later did it become a distinctive marker of plurality. It survives in words such as *feet*, *geese*, *teeth*, *mice*, *lice* and *men*.

As far as the final declension is concerned, it has no interesting survivals in terms of plurality, so let's move on to consider case. I've already shown that other means, such as word order and prepositions, are now being used to express some of the grammatical functions formerly achieved with case. The case that merits our particular attention is the genitive case, since it is from this that we get the apostrophe–*s*. If you look at Table 8.1, you will see that the most common genitive singular marker was the *-es* inflection. This genitive inflection was extended to other nouns, just as the *-as* plural inflection was extended to nouns that originally marked the plural in other ways. In fact, these two inflections merged: by Middle English both were written *-es*. So, for example, OE *hundes* (genitive singular) and OE *hundas* (the plural) both became ME *houndes*. During Middle English virtually all nouns were reduced to two forms: one without *-es* to indicate a singular, and one with *-es* to indicate either a genitive singular or a plural. Most other inflections had died out.

Middle English	Grammatical function	Today's English	Grammatical function
hound(e)	singular	*hound*	singular
hound(e)s	genitive singular	*hound's*	genitive singular
hound(e)s	plural	*hounds*	plural
hound(e)s	genitive plural	*hounds'*	genitive plural

This situation is not so very different from that of today. In *speech*, there are also two forms: so, *hound* has one form without [z] at the end and one with. The idea of using a written apostrophe before the *s* to identify a genitive singular was not adopted until the seventeenth century, and the idea of using it after the *s* to identify a genitive plural was not adopted until the eighteenth century. Today, there is quite a lot of confusion in actual usage.

EXERCISES

8.3 Look through the texts in the 'mini-corpus' and try to find examples of the genitive marked with an *-es* inflection (i.e. nouns to which we would today add an apostophe–*s*).

8.4 Investigate the confusion today about the usage of the apostrophe–*s*. Collect examples of incorrect usage. You are more likely to find them in informal writing. As well as collecting various nouns with the apostrophe–*s*, watch out for that notorious problem: confusion between *its* (= the genitive) and *it's* (= a contraction of *it is*). Does your collection of examples provide evidence that the use of the apostrophe–*s* may be changing?

In this unit, you will have noticed that in terms of inflections English has become a lot simpler. When we look at verbs in the next unit, we will see a very similar situation, and in that unit, I will also comment on why English has lost many of its inflections. You will also have noticed that over time English has come to rely more heavily on word order to do the job inflections once did. English has moved from being an INFLECTIONAL LANGUAGE like Latin to being what is known as an ISOLATING LANGUAGE like Chinese, relying much more on word order to signal grammatical information.

Inflectional language
Isolating language

EXERCISES

8.5 The *s*-genitive (the apostrophe–*s*) does not now behave in quite the same way as an inflection. In Old English the *s*-genitive was an inflection used to indicate the function of the individual words to which it was fixed. In Modern English it has become a grammatical particle that can be freely moved around, and can signal the function of a whole phrase. Thus, in the phrase *the head of department's office* the head of the phrase is *head* (the person who possesses the office), but the apostrophe–*s* is appended to the last word of the phrase *department*. When the *s*-genitive refers to a group of words it is called, sensibly enough, a group-genitive. What is the longest group-genitive you can devise?

8.5 In English there are two ways of expressing possession: the *s*-genitive (e.g. *Jonathan's book*) or using the preposition *of* (e.g. *the book of Jonathan*). Collect examples of the *s*-genitive (possibly drawing upon your collection in Exercise 8.3), and then discover what kinds of noun in today's English tend to carry the *s*-genitive. Consider, for example, whether the noun is animate or inanimate.

How much further do you think this process of inflectional simplification will go? Can we get rid of irregular plurals (e.g. *feet*, *children*) or non-native plurals (e.g. *criteria*, *indices*)? Can we get rid of the apostrophe–*s*? Are there varieties of English where this happens already? If English is simplified, what will be the advantages and for whom? If English is simplified, what will be the disadvantages and for whom?

DISCUSSION POINT

SUMMARY

- The most dramatic change in English grammar has been the loss of inflections. English has moved from being an inflectional language to being an isolating language.
- The inflectional complexity of the past has its legacy in irregular plurals (e.g. *sheep*) and in the apostrophe–*s* of written English.
- Today, there is much confusion over the usage of the apostrophe–*s*.
- Today, personal pronouns are almost as complex as they were in Old English. Second-person pronouns used to be more complex, and in the Early Modern English period were used to signal social information.

FOLLOW-UP READING

Dick Leith's *A Social History of English* (London: Routledge, 1983) contains a readable general overview of the history of English grammar. However, you will need more detail. You could try David Crystal's *Encyclopedia of the English Language* (Cambridge: Cambridge University Press, 1995), pp. 20–1 (Old English grammar), 44–5 (Middle English grammar), 70–1 (Early Modern English grammar) and also 200–3 for some relevant pages on number and the *s*-genitive. Alternatively, you can look up the sections on nouns in a standard historical textbook (e.g. T. Pyles and J. Algeo, *The Origins and Development of the English Language* (Fort Worth, TX: Harcourt Brace Jovanovich, 1993)).

9 GRAMMAR II: VERBS

> As with nouns, verbs have experienced a dramatic loss of inflections. This has been counter-balanced by a rise in the use of auxiliary verbs.

Why is it that to form the past tense of the verb *walk* we add *-ed*, whereas to form the past of the verb *drink* we change the vowel so that we get *drank*? This is one of a number of present-day irregularities in English that can be explained by looking at the development of English. As with nouns, we need to look at how verbs signal their grammatical function, and how this has changed over time.

EXERCISE ✎

9.1 In inflectional terms, present-day English regular verbs are very simple. Take the base or root form of a regular verb (e.g. *walk*). How many different inflections can you put on the end of it? Now, try to work out the grammatical function of each of these inflections (it may help, if you devise short sentences to test the verb form).

Table 9.1 gives an idea of how present-tense verb inflections have changed from Old English to the present day. Where alternative forms exist, they are given in parentheses.

An important point to note is that – as with nouns – the general process over time has been one of simplification, with the gradual erosion of inflections. In fact, the situation used to be even more complicated, because there was also a set of inflections for the past tense. Here I've only shown inflections for the present tense.

54

Table 9.1   Old English present tense verb inflections

Number	Person	Today	Early Modern English	Middle English (Midlands)	Old English
Singular	1st I	walk	sit	thanke	drife
	2nd you	walk	sittest	thankest	drifest
	3rd he/she/it	walks	sitteth (-s)	thanketh (-es)	drifeð
Plural	1st we	walk	sit	thanke(n) (-es)	drifað
	2nd you	walk	sit	thanke(n) (-es)	drifað
	3rd they	walk	sit	thanke(n) (-es)	drifað

Let's start by focusing on the one remaining inflection for person in today's English, the *-s* of the third person singular. In fact, in some varieties of today's English – some dialects of East Anglia, for example – even this inflection has been lost. If you look down the line to the far right, you'll see that in Old English there was no *-s*, but instead an *eð*. (Remember that the *ð* character was later replaced by *th*). In Middle English we get both forms. Note that here I am representing the Midlands dialect. (Chaucer wrote in what was essentially the East Midlands dialect.) Differences between dialects in Middle English were much greater than now, as we shall see in the next unit. Why did the *-s* suddenly appear as an option in the Middle English Midlands dialect? To answer this we must look further north. The Scandinavians who settled in the north had provided English with the *-s* inflection. Over time this spread southwards through the rest of the country. By the Early Modern English period the *-eth* inflection was in serious decline, and came to be seen as rather archaic. It survived longest in the words *hath* and *doth* which are still found in the eighteenth century.

━━━━━━━━━━━━━━━━━━━━━━━━━━━━━━━━━━━━━━━ **EXERCISE** ✎

9.2   Note examples of *-eth* or *-s* in the 'mini-corpus' in Appendix III. In particular, can you explain why Text 6, the Authorised Version of the Bible, is dominated by *-eth*?

━━━━━━━━━━━━━━━━━━━━━━━━━━━━━━━━━━━━━━━

Let's turn to tense. We noted earlier that the regular way of forming the past tense in English is simply to add the inflection *-ed*. However, there are a number of irregular verbs. English, in common with other Germanic languages, divides its verbs into two groups – so-called weak and strong – according to how they form their past tense and past participle. [If you are not clear about what a past participle is, make sure that you have read the description given in the answer to Exercise 9.1.]

Weak verbs add a *-d* or *-t* to the root in order to form the past or the past participle, for example:

Present	Past	Past participle
kiss	kissed	kissed
fill	filled	filled
build	built	built
hear	heard	heard

The vast majority of verbs in English form their past and past participles in this way.

Strong verbs do not add an inflection, but change the vowel of their base form:

Present	Past	Past participle
ride	rode	ridden
speak	spoke	spoken
see	saw	seen
drink	drank	drunk

All strong-verb past participles originally had the inflection *-en* at the end and also *ge-* at the beginning. So, in Old English the past participle of the verb *ride* is *geriden*.

EXERCISE ✎

9.3 Old forms of participles have survived in some contexts. Where might you hear:

    drunken as opposed to *drunk*

    molten as opposed to *melted*

    stricken as opposed to *struck*

    shrunken as opposed to *shrunk*

One should bear in mind here that not all speakers of English make the same distinctions between the past and past participle, often using one form for both. Thus, today many speakers of English use *done* as both past participle (*It was done well*) and simple past (*She done well*), and many are using *drunk* for the simple past (e.g. *She drunk the milk*). These variations reflect a general process of REGULARISATION or simplification of verb forms.

Regularisation

    The most important change to these weak and strong verb patterns is the conversion of the minority of strong verbs to the weak pattern. According to one estimate, five-sixths of the 360 or so strong verbs have changed. At various points in time, you can find both strong and weak forms of a verb. Thus, in the sixteenth century you can find both *laughed – low, crept – crope, helped – holp*.

EXERCISE ✎

9.4 Which of the following pairs would you use: *dived – dove*, *hanged – hung*, *weaved – wove*, *strived – strove*, *digged – dug*? Would you use both, but in different contexts?

It's worth noting that all new verbs follow the *-ed* weak pattern. In other words, if we want to indicate the past tense or make a participle, we put an *-ed* on the end of the word. For example, a British television advertisement for the soft drink *Tango* converts the brand name into a verb and makes it a past participle by adding *-ed*: *You know when you've been tangoe'd.*

Let's turn to AUXILIARY VERBS. What are auxiliary verbs? Let's introduce a distinction between MAIN VERBS and auxiliary verbs by way of some examples:

Auxiliary verbs
Main verbs

(1) I *may* drive

(2) I *do* not drive

(3) It *is being* driven

   It *has been being* driven

In each case the main verb is *drive*. The italicised auxiliary verbs help the main verb in some particular way; they perform functions that in other languages might be performed by inflections. I'm going to focus on the use of *do* as an auxiliary verb, as illustrated in example (2). However, a general point to note about auxiliary verbs is that the further you go back in time the less likely you are to find a series of auxiliary verbs. In fact, neither of the examples in (3) above existed in Early Modern English, and the final (admittedly rare) example *It **has been being** driven* is a twentieth-century development.

The development of the auxiliary verb *do* represents one of the most important changes in the English language. Today, it can be used as an auxiliary in a variety of ways: for emphasis in statements (e.g. *They do look for trouble*), to form a negative statement (e.g. *They do not look for trouble*), and in questions (e.g. *Do they look for trouble?*). In Old English the use of *do* was somewhat different. As a main verb, it seems to have originally meant 'to put or place something somewhere': 'ðæt mon his sweord *doo* ofer his hype' (King Ælfred, *Gregory's Past*, 897) (= literally, that man his sword places over his hip). Indeed, *do* can still be used as a main verb today with the sense of 'putting', 'giving' or 'performing'. Consider: *to do to death*, *to do someone credit*, *to do some work*. It was not until Middle English that it developed as a common auxiliary.

From Late Middle English (fourteenth to fifteenth centuries) *do* became popular as a 'dummy' auxiliary, that is to say, an empty or meaningless auxiliary. It was particularly popular in Early Modern English. Sometimes *do* was used somewhat like today to add emphasis in statements, but often it served no particular function. [Check Texts 5 and 6 for examples of 'dummy' *do*.] If you interpret every example of *do* in Shakespeare as adding emphasis, you will be misreading Shakespeare, particularly as Shakespeare and other literary writers often used *do* if they needed an extra syllable to make up a metrical line.

The typical way of forming questions in Old English had been to reverse the normal subject–verb order. This question-forming method was still used in Early Modern English. Thus, Shakespeare could write 'Spake you of Caesar?' (*Antony and Cleopatra* III.ii.11), reversing the normal order for a statement: *You* (subject) *spake* (verb) *of Caesar*. But by Shakespeare's time questions were being formed simply by placing *do* before the subject: 'Do you see this?' (*Hamlet* IV.v.197). [Check Text 5(c) for examples of questions formed in these different ways.]

In Old English, negative statements could be formed by supplying the word *ne* (usually before the verb): 'he *ne* iaf him al' (Peterborough Chronicle, 1140) (= he did not give him all). They could also be formed by adding *ne* before the verb and *not* after: '*Ne* con ic *noht* singan' (King Ælfred, *Cædmon's Hymn*, ninth century) (= I know not [how] to sing). In Middle English *ne* ceased to be used, leaving just *not*: 'they were not gylty' (William Soper, late fifteenth century). This method of forming negative statements carries on well into the Early Modern English period. But at this time we also find *do* being used. So, in John Bunyan's *The Pilgrim's Progress* (1678) we can read both 'I care not what I meet' and 'I did not put the question to thee.' [Check Texts 3, 6 and 7 for examples of negative statements formed without *do*.]

In this and the last unit, we have seen some radical changes in English in the way inflections of words have been lost. But why did English lose them? [Refer back to the possible reasons for language change given towards the end of **Unit 2**.] English underwent a phonological change leading to a grammatical change: the inflections at the ends of many words ceased to be stressed, and were thus liable to blend with other inflections and disappear altogether (since people could not hear them so well). Furthermore, given that British English has experienced contact with an array of different languages (i.e. Celtic, Scandinavian and French), there may well have been pressure for regularisation, in order to make it easier for people to communicate. Outside Britain, English – as we shall see in **Unit 12** – has come into contact with many languages, creating yet further pressure to simplify the inflectional system.

DISCUSSION POINT

Note that, as in the example from Ælfred above, a regular way of forming a negative statement in the past has been to use more than one negative word. In what varieties of today's English are you more likely to meet double or multiple negatives? What are the social implications of using double or multiple negatives? Is there any *linguistic* reason why they are a problem (consider whether communication is impaired or made more effective)?

SUMMARY

- Today, there is one remaining inflection for person, the *-s*, which is a Scandinavian borrowing. The Anglo-Saxon inflection used in Old English, the *-eth*, lingered on until the eighteenth century.
- The presence today of a number of verbs that form their past and past participles in an irregular way (i.e. not with an *-ed* inflection) can be explained by examining the development of weak verbs and strong verbs. The strong-verb pattern has become increasingly rare. In a few cases, a verb has both strong and weak forms (e.g. *hung – hanged*).
- Auxiliary verbs have played an increasingly important role in English. Today, it is not unusual to have two or more auxiliary verbs in a row.
- The auxiliary *do* has had a profound effect on the development of English grammar, playing a role in forming emphatic statements, questions and negative statements.
- Two explanations have been put forward for the dramatic loss of inflections in English: (1) the loss of distinctiveness in pronunciation, due to the fact that the inflections were unstressed; and (2) the regularisation of inflections to facilitate communication between peoples speaking different languages and dialects.

FOLLOW-UP READING

The same readings mentioned in the last unit from Dick Leith's *A Social History of English* (London: Routledge, 1983) and David Crystal's *Encyclopedia of the English Language* (Cambridge: Cambridge University Press, 1995) are also relevant to this unit. In addition, pp. 204–5 and 212 in Crystal's *Encyclopedia* contain relevant general information on verbs, and, of course, you can look up the sections on verbs in a standard historical textbook (e.g. T. Pyles and J. Algeo, *The Origins and Development of the English Language* (Fort Worth, TX: Harcourt Brace Jovanovich, 1993)).

10 DIALECTS IN BRITISH ENGLISH

> Dialects in Britain can be explained with reference to the presence and movement of various peoples, as well as the fact that language change took place at different speeds for different groups.

Eleven years ago I arrived in the city of Lancaster in the north-west of England, having travelled up from London, where I was born and bred. Now, the speech of most of the north-west, is fairly familiar to me, but at the time I was struck by what I heard. The word *book* sounded like [buːk], not [bʊk]. People would tell me that they want something *fixing*, rather than they want something *fixed*. And where was I going, if I went up a *ginnel*? (A *ginnel* turned out to be a narrow passageway between buildings.) What I was experiencing was a different DIALECT, a different regional dialect. The term dialect refers to a variety of language characterised in terms of pronunciation, grammar and lexis; the term ACCENT refers to a variety of language characterised in terms of pronunciation only.

Dialect

Accent

People from the United States are sometimes struck by the variety and distinctiveness of dialects in Britain. If you live in the west of the United States, you could journey for days without hearing a strikingly unusual pronunciation or expression. But in Britain, a day's journey could lead you through a rich and varied tapestry of sounds, structures and words. In fact, if you go back in time, the regional differences between dialects are even more dramatic.

EXERCISE

10.1 Can you think of features of your dialect that make it distinctive, features that contrast with the features of dialects in other places? Try to find features at each linguistic level: grammatical,

lexical and phonological (i.e. pronunciation). So, for example, someone who says *he say it* (as opposed to *he says it*) may well come from
Norfolk; someone who says *bairn* (as opposed to *child*) may well come
from the far north of England or Scotland; and someone who pro-
nounces the word *singer* as [sɪŋɡə] (as opposed to [sɪŋə]) may well
come from west central England (e.g. Birmingham, Manchester,
Liverpool).

Let's start by considering the arrival of English in Britain. You will
remember from **Unit 1** that various Germanic tribes – the Angles,
the Saxons and the Jutes – began to settle in Britain in the fifth
century. The Angles settled in and gave their name to what is now
East Anglia, and also spread to Mercia (the Midlands) and further
north to Northumbria (north of the Humber and south-east
Scotland). The Saxons remained in the south, a fact evidenced by
the area names *Sussex* (= south Saxons), *Essex* (= east Saxons), and
the old name for the south-west *Wessex* (= west Saxons). The Jutes
seem to have remained largely in Kent. Some of the dialectal differences in today's English may originate in the Germanic dialects
spoken by these tribes. Map 10.1 shows what are believed to be the
Old English dialect areas.

As you can see, there are four main dialects: (1) *Northumbrian* –
north of the Humber and south-east Scotland; (2) *Mercian or Midland*
– further to the south and containing two main subdialects, West
Midland and East Midland; (3) *Kentish* – the south-east (including
modern Kent and Surrey); and (4) *West Saxon* – south of the Thames,
from Sussex to Devon, but excluding the Cornish-speaking area.
Sometimes Northumbrian and Mercian are grouped together as
Anglian. In fact, some of the Old English dialect boundaries coincide
with today's dialect boundaries. From the point of view of today's
accents, an important boundary is that between Northumbrian and
Mercian. Below a line roughly from the mouth of the river Humber
to the mouth of the river Lune near Lancaster, you can find, for
example, *ground* pronounced [graʊnd], *blind* pronounced [blaɪnd]
and *wrong* pronounced [rɒŋ]. However, above that line you are more
likely to find them pronounced [grʊnd], [blɪnd] and [raŋ].

In **Unit 1**, we have seen how the Scandinavians settled in the north
and east of England in the Old English period, and how the
Scandinavian language, Old Norse, influenced placenames in those
regions. Although Old Norse and English were not distantly related
languages and were to a degree mutually comprehensible, the presence of Norse in Britain sharpened the distinction between northern
and southern varieties of English. Do you remember Caxton's eggs
story in Text 3? The communication problem can be explained by
noting that *egges* is a Norse loanword, and *eyren* is an Old English
word. At the time the story takes place, in the fifteenth century,
egges had worked its way down and was well established in London;
but further south in Kent *eyren* was still current.

MAP 10.1   Old English dialect areas

EXERCISE ✎

10.2   All of the words given below are typically found in the north of England. Use a dictionary to find out the etymology of these words, noting down the language from which they are borrowed. It will also be interesting to note down equivalent forms, if they are listed, in today's Scandinavian languages (e.g. Danish, Norwegian, Swedish). Present your results in a table, so that by looking across a row you can get a sense of how similar these northern dialectal words are to those in Scandinavian languages.

garth	(yard)	laik	(to play)
kist	(chest)	tarn	(small mountain lake)
nay	(no)	kirk	(church)
steg	(gander)	nieve	(fist)
smoot	(narrow passage)	fell	(hill, mountain)
beck	(brook)	addle	(to acquire)

As we have already noted during the course of this book, the Middle English period was one of variety, including great regional variety. Let's not forget that a number of languages were used in Britain at this time: Latin was used for formal texts (e.g. laws, religious texts, scholarly works), Norman French was used for administration and spoken by the upper classes, whilst English became a set of largely spoken dialects, except in Cornwall, Wales and Scotland, where Celtic languages were spoken. As Map 10.2 shows, the English dialect areas were very similar to those of Old English, except that West and East Midlands are regarded as distinct dialects in their own right. There is no one principal dialect in Middle English. In fact, important Middle English texts survive in all five dialects. That is because there was no generally accepted written standard. As we saw in **Unit 3**, if people wrote in English, they wrote as they would speak.

We have seen how some English dialects partly developed their distinctiveness because they came into contact with languages (e.g. Norse) which other parts of the country did not. But this is only part of the story of English dialects. Variation also comes about when the dialectal features of different speakers develop at different speeds. Let's look at accents in particular and consider the dramatic changes in long vowels that took place in Early Modern English. You may remember that these changes were referred to as the 'Great Vowel Shift' in **Unit 3**. [Turn back and reread the relevant paragraph now.] Take as an example the pronunciation of the word *house*. The chart below suggests how the pronunciation of *house* has changed over time. Practise the pronunciations given. [Check the symbols in Appendix II, so that you can be sure what sounds they represent.]

The changing pronunciation of 'house'

	Old English	Middle English	Early Modern English	Today?
house	huːs	huːs	həʊs	haʊs

When you say [uː], think about where the vowel is articulated in your mouth (try comparing it with the word *sweet*, the vowel of which we concluded in **Unit 3** was articulated high at the front of the mouth). You should find that it is right at the back of your mouth and right at the top (compare with the back vowel [ɑ] which is articulated low in the mouth). If it is the case, as stated in **Unit 3**, that

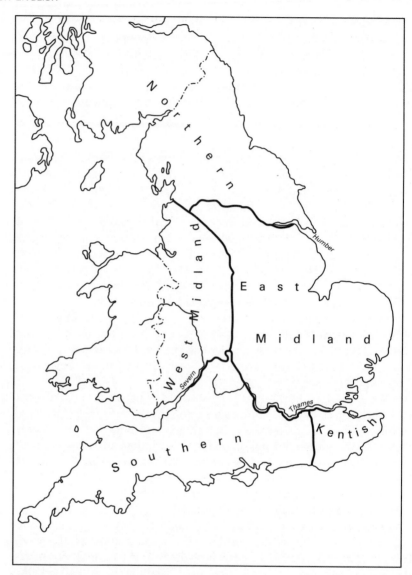

MAP 10.2 Middle English dialect areas

Diphthong

the Great Vowel Shift involved back vowels moving up and back, then what is to happen to [uː]? The answer is that if a vowel is already at the top, then it becomes a DIPHTHONG – two vowel sounds run together, so that you begin with one and finish with the other. So, [uː] changed to the diphthong [əʊ], and then [ɑʊ]. Has change stopped here? Let's consider popular London speech, which, in some respects, has undergone greater change than other accents. Here, the diphthong [ɑʊ] in words like *house* and *town* seems to have developed yet further, losing the [u] quality, so that pronunciations more like [taːn] with a monophthong can be heard.

EXERCISES ✎

10.3 Have a guess at the exercises below. Don't panic, if you feel that English dialects are something of a mystery. You can find some answers in Appendix IV.

(a) Where in Britain has the pronunciation of the vowel [uː] in words such as *house* not undergone the changes mapped out above?

(b) In **Unit 8** we looked at the use of second-person pronouns and, in particular, the use of *you* and *thou* forms in Early Modern English. It is not the case, however, that *thou* forms have completely died out. Where in Britain can you still hear the *thou* forms of the second-person pronoun?

(c) Where in Britain can you still hear the *r* pronounced after a vowel in words like *car* and *farm* (this feature of people's speech is sometimes referred to as a 'burr')? Three hundred years ago POST-VOCALIC R was pronounced throughout England, but began to rapidly disappear in the south-east from the eighteenth century.

Post-vocalic *r*

(d) Over the last few centuries, a new vowel sound [ʌ] in words such as *much*, *sun* and *money* has developed, particularly in the accent of speakers in the London region. Where in Britain is this vowel not used? What vowel is used to replace it in words such as those above?

(e) Over the last few centuries, the vowel sound [æ] in words such as *bath*, *grass* and *dance* has changed to [ɑː], particularly in the accent of speakers in the London region. Where in Britain has this change not taken place?

10.4 What do you think the areas you have identified in the above exercises in 10.3 have in common? Why is it that change has not occurred here and why has it occurred in other parts of Britain?

So far, we have been investigating the development of traditional dialects. Traditional dialects are what people usually think about when they consider dialects. They tend to be frequently stereotyped. The south-western English dialect has been unfairly and often inaccurately caricatured on stage, since at least the time of Shakespeare. Whilst these dialects are still important, and are particularly apparent amongst older people in rural areas, we cannot ignore the effect of improved communications. In fact, the frequent complaint today that 'dialects are dying out' reflects the fact that the basis for dialects has shifted. A hundred and fifty years ago the vast majority of the population lived and died without travelling further than a few miles. Communities were thus relatively isolated: they didn't come into contact with speakers of other dialects. Now, people regularly travel hundreds of miles and think nothing of it. People commute to work in London from as far afield as Birmingham. Such mobility would explain, for example, why 150 years ago there was a traditional Kentish dialect, whilst today it barely survives. Of course, this is not to say that traditional dialects are replaced by nothing. Relatively new dialect forms based on urban areas have become influential, spreading outwards from urban centres and particularly down lines of communication. The spread of regional London speech, something which has in fact been happening for centuries, has recently attracted media attention, and the variety of English concerned has been given the jazzy title of 'Estuary English' (after the river Thames estuary). Evidence of Estuary English has been found in areas of Hull, Chester and Bristol – all of which have good communication links with London. Typical features of popular London speech include the use of glottal stops (especially replacing [t] at the end of a word or before a consonant, e.g. *treatment*); the pronunciation of *l* in words like *hill*, so that it sounds more like [w]; the use of *never* as in *No I never*; the absence of the adverb ending *-ly* as in *I did it quick*.

DISCUSSION POINT

In this unit we have attempted to examine the history of dialects from a purely descriptive point of view. However, in everyday life people are as likely – or more likely – to make social judgements about regional dialects as they are to describe them. Which stereotypical characteristics are often attached to which dialect? If you are part of a group, try to come to an agreement about associations of various dialects. To help you, think about the use of dialects in plays or films: which dialects are used to create rustic, 'country bumpkin' characters, which dialects are used for shifty, small-time gangsters and which dialects are used for people in a position of power?

You will probably be able to generate a fairly rich collection of associations for the dialects you choose. These are purely social judgements: there is no linguistic reason why one dialect suggests one thing and another something else. But, of course, such judgements are an unfortunate fact of the world around us. What implications do such judgements have for, say, the selection of someone for a job, the treatment of children in a classroom or the election of someone for a government post? We will return to the notion of dialect and social judgement in the following unit.

SUMMARY

- Britain has considerable diversity in its dialects, and this diversity begins with the arrival of the Angles, Saxons and Jutes speaking various Germanic dialects.
- Old English saw four main dialect areas (Northumbrian, Mercian, Kentish and West Saxon) established, and these are very similar to those of Middle English. Today, some of these boundaries are still important dialectal boundaries.

- The settlement of the north and east of Britain by Scandinavians speaking Norse resulted in a sharpening of the distinction between northern and southern varieties of English.
- The fact that the dialects developed at different speeds resulted in further variation. For example, not all dialects experienced the full set of changes that took place during the Great Vowel Shift.
- In a number of respects, London has been at the forefront of change.
- More recently, urban dialects have become increasingly important, and these have tended to spread out along lines of communication.

The relevant pages on British English dialects in David Crystal's *Encyclopedia of the English Language* (Cambridge: Cambridge University Press, 1995) are pp. 28–9, 50–1 and 324–7. Also, it's worth reading the pages on English in Scotland (pp. 328–33), Wales (pp. 334–5) and Ireland (pp. 336–7). For a historical perspective, the book usually consulted is M.F. Wakelin's *English Dialects: an Introduction* (London: Athlone Press, 1972). For present-day considerations of dialect, try P. Trudgill's *Dialects* (London: Routledge, 1994), a book which is part of the same series as this one, or A. Hughes and P. Trudgill, *English Accents and Dialects* (2nd edn, London: Edward Arnold, 1987).

FOLLOW-UP READING

11 STANDARDISATION

> The development of 'standard' English proceeded along very different lines for speech and writing, and thus they are considered separately here.

At the moment, my car needs two new tyres. The car itself was manufactured in Italy and the tyres in France. But I am confident that I could go down to my local garage in the north-west of England and be able to buy some suitable tyres. Why? Because tyres are manufactured throughout Europe, and in many other countries besides, according to a standard set of sizes. In fact, mass production, as in the automobile industry, relies on standardisation when it comes to assembling components from a variety of different suppliers: the bolts must be the right size for the holes in the chassis, the nuts must be threaded the right way for the bolts, the spanners must be the right size for the nuts, and so on.

In *written* English too there is a certain standard. We do not normally spel werds enihau, make up snooky words or use structures grammatical strange, because this would make communication more difficult. In the fifteenth century, William Caxton was also aware of this issue. In the *egges* story in Text 3, Caxton bewails the lack of an agreed standard in the Middle English period, and we have seen during the course of this book how variation occurred at every linguistic level. Rather like the automobile industry, Caxton's wish for some kind of standard had an economic dimension. Clearly, it would be very costly to print a different version of a book for every variety of English. So, Caxton needed to pick one variety of English that was widely understood and was socially valued. Let's consider some possible choices.

John of Trevisa put his finger on one possible choice. [Reread Text 2.] The dialects of the middle of England were more likely to be understood by people to either side. Thus, this would suggest a Midlands dialect. What about a dialect that was socially valued? It so happened that the dialect of London was essentially that of the East Midlands, and London had the prestige of being the capital city, the political centre and the centre of commerce and administration. We have already noted in the previous unit the great influence London had and has on the development of dialects.

However, whilst we might consider possible choices for Caxton, to some extent the choice had already been made. From the arrival of the Normans up until about 1430, all official documentation was written in French or Latin. During the fourteenth century, the prestige of French became somewhat reduced, at least amongst some sectors of the population, for political reasons: from 1337, England had been engaged in the so-called 'Hundred Years War' with France. Moreover, by the fifteenth century, the administrative system needed an efficient medium for communication, not a language understood by a very small elite. The Chancery or government scribes adopted a variety of English that was based on London, but with some central Midland elements, and this variety has been called the CHANCERY STANDARD. The significance of this is that at that point we have an institution producing masses of paperwork in one variety of English which is then sent all over the country. Caxton set up his printing press in Westminster in 1476, close to the government offices. His adoption of a London-based variety of English, including some features of the English of official circles, was the obvious choice.

Chancery standard

EXERCISE ✎

11.1 It is a mistake to think that standard written English is centred on a southern variety of English. London, though geographically quite far south in England, was actually within the Midlands dialect boundary. Moreover, the final written standard that emerges contains some important northern features, but lacks some important southern features. Take as an example today's third person plural pronouns *they*, *them* and *their*. These are descended from the northern forms, and are ultimately Scandinavian in origin. The equivalent southern forms were *hi*, *him* and *hire*.

(a) One of the most important inflections in standard written English was originally a northern form. What is it?
(b) Some core vocabulary items were originally northern words. Give some examples.

(*Hint:* Some answers to these questions are in **Units 4 and 9**. Think about features which are originally Scandinavian.)

The fact that printers, like Caxton, adopted a particular variety of English obviously did much to promote it, since they had the ability to mass-produce it. But other factors were involved in the creation of a recognised national standard of written English. Remember, for example, that one of the most prestigious domains of written language usage – religion – was still dominated by an entirely different language, namely Latin. A political move that led to change here was the Reformation: Henry VIII's split from the Roman Catholic Church in 1533. One way of challenging the power of the Catholic Church, which operated in Latin throughout Europe, was to produce texts in English. The first licensed English Bible appeared in 1537 and the Book of Common Prayer – a service book for the Church of England – in 1549. The most famous English Bible, promoted by James I, appeared in 1611. [You can see extracts from the 1611 Authorised Version of the Bible in Text 6.] All this had the effect of increasing a national focus on English. Perhaps more importantly, what finally fixed the standard in the minds of users was the growth of dictionaries, grammar books, spelling books, and so on from the sixteenth century onwards. These were adopted in schools, and became arbiters of the language. They CODIFIED the standard by offering an authoritative consensus about what the standard consisted of.

Codified

The fact that various individuals, such as Jonathan Swift, set themselves up as authorities on the English language and wrote books often with the explicit aim of setting a standard variety of English in concrete has important implications for today's users of the language. We all consult authoritative sources, typically dictionaries, for word meanings, spellings, grammatical points, and so on. We've already seen the limitations of dictionaries in **Unit 6**. During the 'Discussion point' of **Unit 2**, I'm sure that many 'rules', perhaps learnt from past teachers, will have come to light. In fact, many of these rules can be traced back to the eighteenth century (a bonanza century for making rules) or earlier. Unfortunately, many of these rules lack a sound basis: they reflect an appeal to pseudo-logic or to etymology, a wish to emulate the prestigious language Latin, or simply the whim of the writer.

EXERCISE ✎

11.21

(a) Is it really possible to 'fix the language' to a certain standard, as many commentators in the eighteenth century wished to do?

(b) Below is a set of examples that would have troubled an eighteenth-century writer and are still hot issues today. What 'rule' is broken in each example and can you imagine why the 'rule' was devised?

(1) Tom, ill upstairs, complained to his mother: 'What did you bring that book I didn't want to be read to out of up for?'

(2) ... the voyages of the starship Enterprise, its con-
tinuing mission:
to explore strange new worlds,
to seek out new life and new civilisations,
to boldly go where no one has gone before.'

(3) Share it among the two of you.

(4) I never did nothing.

So far, we've discussed the development of a written standard; we must now consider the possibility of a spoken standard. Can we today speak of a spoken 'standard'? Is there an accent – a variety of language characterised solely in terms of pronunciation – that matches the standard of written language? Is there an accent used by the vast majority of people and one that enjoys high prestige? Clearly, there is no one accent used by the majority of speakers. Even small groups of people are likely to have speakers of different accents. So, unlike the written standard, with speech there can be no notion of a majority form. However, we can talk about a prestige form. I'm sure that even non-British readers will have heard of the Queen's English, BBC English or simply 'talking posh'. Linguists sometimes refer to this accent as RECEIVED PRONUNCIATION (RP) ('received' has the earlier sense of 'accepted').

Received Pronunciation (RP)

For centuries, people have made aesthetic and social judgements about accents. [See, for example, Trevisa's comments on the Yorkshire accent in Text 2.] From the sixteenth century onwards, a growing number of writers designated the speech of the upper classes and, in particular, of the court in London as a prestige form. For example, George Puttenham (1589) advises the poet to use 'the usuall speach of the Court, and that of London and the shires about London within lx. myles, and not much above'. With royalty sited at London and a 60 mile radius including the important cultural centres Cambridge, Oxford and Canterbury, it is not a surprise that the prestige form was based here. In the nineteenth century, this form was firmly established as the accent of the ruling classes through the public-school system. Those who could afford to send their children to public schools did so in the expectation that they would experience the accent so strongly associated with the upper classes, in other words, Received Pronunciation. Scholars have argued that one effect of this was to break down the regional associations of RP: an RP speaker from the south would sound similar to an RP speaker from the north, because they had been through the same education system. Today, although the majority of RP speakers live in the south-east of England, it is the case that the non-localised nature of RP is one of its characteristics: if you hear an RP speaker, you may guess their social background, but not where they come from.

Two other factors played a role in establishing the dominance of RP. Just as technology – the printing presses – had played a role in establishing a written standard, so technology was to play a role in promoting a particular accent. With the advent of radio broadcasting in the 1920s, the BBC needed to formulate a policy as to what variety of spoken English they would use, and they chose RP. The second factor was that RP was codified by British linguists in the twentieth century. It is the pronunciation given in dictionaries of English and taught to foreign learners of British English. More has been written about RP than any other accent. This is an odd state of affairs, if one considers that RP is a minority accent spoken today by around 3–5 per cent of the population of Britain.

Of course, the correlation of certain accents with certain classes is entirely a social matter. It has nothing to do with particular accents being linguistically better. However, this has not stopped people from evaluating others on the basis of the way they speak. RP, as well as the written standard, is sometimes used as a 'standard' for judging people, so that 'non-standard' is taken to mean deficient in some way. This everyday notion of 'standard' has no linguistic justification at all. For example, a commonly held idea is that non-RP speakers are 'lazy' or 'slovenly', because they don't pronounce all the letters in words. If you think about it, this idea doesn't match the facts. We saw in **Unit 3** how *nobody* would pronounce all the letters in a word. Moreover, RP speakers too use reduced forms (e.g. no RP speaker would pronounce 'and' as [ænd], but much more likely [ən]) and drop letters (e.g. the *t* in the phrase *soft pillow*). Indeed, there is no simplistic equation such that the more sounds we supply in pronouncing a word the higher up the social scale it will be rated. Consider the pronunciation of the word *sing*. The RP pronunciation is [sɪŋ], a regional (west central England) pronunciation is [sɪŋg]. It is the regional pronunciation that has more phonemes and more closely reflects the spelling of the word.

Today, RP has less authority than it used to have in the first half of the twentieth century. It is less widely used now. People still strongly associate it with high social status, but it does not have quite the prestige it once had. It is often referred to as 'plummy', 'stuck up' or 'contrived', and closely identifies a speaker with the establishment – something that might well be a negative feature, par-

Modified RP

ticularly for younger people. MODIFIED RP, a mixture of RP and regional features, is becoming more common. An interesting development has been the move by some RP speakers towards Estuary English. In fact, Estuary English has been described as lying in the middle of a scale with RP at one end and popular London speech at the other (or, as one newspaper put it, 'between Cockney and the Queen'). Estuary English seems to have more prestige than RP, especially amongst young people. Thus, Nigel Kennedy, a violinist with a RP-speaking background, speaks Estuary English: a good vehicle for popularising classical music.

11.3   What are the factors that lead to the standardisation of a particular accent or dialect?

11.4   How helpful is the 'tyres' analogy with which I open this unit? In what ways might it be misleading or a distortion of the notion of 'standard' when applied to language?

11.5   Many people, particularly politicians and the media, are notorious for their (wilful?) misunderstanding of the concept of 'standard' when it is applied to language. Part of the problem lies in an everyday usage of the word *standard*. Describe the nature of this misunderstanding, and the kind of abuse it can lead to.

11.6   In the past, the British royal family have been the stronghold of RP, but this seems to be changing. Younger members (e.g. Prince Andrew, Prince Edward) have distinctly different accents from the older members (e.g. the Queen, Prince Charles). In particular, the influence on the speech of the younger members seems to be coming from Estuary English. Try to tape any news reports, interviews, speeches or documentaries involving members of the royal family. Then compare the speech of individuals, looking out for typical features of Estuary English (see the previous unit). An interesting extension of this study would be to compare old recordings of the royal family (e.g. the queen's coronation) with present-day recordings, and to note any changes that have occurred. (Remember that such old recordings are often available in public libraries.) The kind of features of conservative RP which you might listen out for include: *off* pronounced as [ɔːf] and not [ɒf]; the vowel of *cat* pronounced so that it rhymes more closely with *bet* than *bat*; and the second vowel of *refined* pronounced so that it rhymes more closely with *rained* than *rind*.

DISCUSSION POINT

As far as language is concerned, what 'standard' should be taught in schools? Need a 'standard' be taught at all? In England this has been the subject of much debate. What should a teacher do, if a child writes a non-standard spelling? What should a teacher do, if a child uses non-standard grammar and lexis in writing? What should a teacher do, if a child uses a regional pronunciation? Consider also the possibility that there might be different solutions for different situations or different types of writing. If you are part of a group, you can set up a debate revolving around certain options.

SUMMARY

- The written standard emerges in the fifteenth century and is a development of the London dialect, which is itself based on the East Midlands dialect. Such a dialect was an effective medium for communication between north and south, and had the prestige of being the dialect of the capital.
- The adoption of a London-based variety for the administrative system and its uptake by printers such as Caxton were important factors in establishing the written standard. From the sixteenth century onwards the standard was codified.
- A prestige accent based on the court and the London area clearly emerges in the sixteenth century.
- The public-school system established RP as the dominant high-class accent. RP was promoted with the advent of broadcasting, and it was codified in the twentieth century. However, over the last few years RP has experienced something of a decline.
- The notion of 'standard' is very problematic. Clearly, the 'standard' in writing is different from the 'standard' in speech, and what the general public understand by 'standard' may yet be something else.

FOLLOW-UP READING

The relevant pages on standardisation in David Crystal's *Encyclopedia of the English Language* (Cambridge: Cambridge University Press, 1995) are pp. 54–5 on the written standard and p. 365 on RP. It is also worth reading pp. 110–11 and 113. Here the notion of 'standard English' and of a 'world standard English' is considered. World Englishes will be the topic of the next unit. In addition, most of the standard books on dialects (see the previous unit) or on the general history of the English language will include a section on the standardisation of English.

WORLD ENGLISHES

12

> The crucial factor in the development of English over the last few centuries is its role in the world. English has been brought into contact with new environments and languages, and as a result has developed in new directions, giving rise to different varieties of English.

English has gone global. Today, English dominates the world stage in a number of language uses: it is the main language of publishing, science, technology, commerce, diplomacy, air-traffic control and popular music. The reasons for this are to do with the political and economic power of Britain in the nineteenth century and the United States in the twentieth century. These same reasons also account for a dramatic increase in the number of users of English. In the sixteenth century there were approximately 3 million speakers of English. Today, there are over 300 million native speakers of English. To this, one could add a further 300 million who regularly speak English as a second language (i.e. in addition to their native language). In fact, it has been estimated that in total around a billion people use English with varying degrees of proficiency. English is the most widely used language in the world.

EXERCISE ✎

12.1

    (a) List as many countries as you can where English is spoken as a native language (ENL countries).

    (b) List as many countries as you can where English is spoken as a second language (ESL countries). Such countries usually give English some kind of official status; English may be used for administrative and legal purposes, or in certain newspapers; and often these countries were formerly part of the British Empire.

(c) List a selection of countries where English is spoken as a foreign language (EFL countries).

World Englishes

With the international spread of English it is perhaps more appropriate now to speak of WORLD ENGLISHES. American and British English are the two most important national varieties, in terms both of numbers of speakers and of world-wide impact (Britain through its former Empire, and North America through its economic power), so let's consider them in more detail. Why did the different varieties develop? Early in the seventeenth century the first settlements from Britain were established in North America. Separated from England, brought into contact with a new environment and native Indian languages, it is not surprising that American English acquired its own characteristics.

EXERCISE ✎

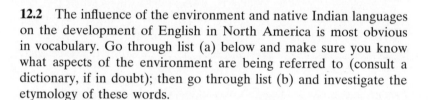

12.2   The influence of the environment and native Indian languages on the development of English in North America is most obvious in vocabulary. Go through list (a) below and make sure you know what aspects of the environment are being referred to (consult a dictionary, if in doubt); then go through list (b) and investigate the etymology of these words.

(a) *back country, bluff, garter-snake, groundhog, notch* (as a landscape feature), *prairie*
(b) *canoe, chipmunk, moose, racoon, toboggan, tapioca*

It is sometimes said that American English still has features which are archaic from the point of view of British English. Let's take some features of General American English (hereafter GA) – what is sometimes described as the 'standard' American dialect and accent, typically found in the middle states and in the west – and compare them with the language of a British RP speaker.

- In GA the vowel in words such as *ask, dance, bath* and *half* is [æ], not [ɑː] as in RP. The [æ] began to be lost in southern British English from the late eighteenth century.
- In GA the letter *r* is pronounced in all positions, but in RP it is only pronounced before vowels (e.g. *very, paragraph*). It is claimed that post-vocalic *r* began to disappear from London speech from the late seventeenth century.
- In RP the vowels in pairs like *cot/caught* are distinct: [ɒ] and [ɔː] respectively. However, in GA these vowels have merged in various ways. For example, in south-western American speech [ɑ] is used in both *cot* and *caught*. This

is similar to an older pronunciation in British English: note that Chaucer spelt 'not' as *nat*.

- Perhaps the most striking morphological difference between GA and British English is the use of the past participle form *gotten* in GA. This was in fact the usual form in British English two centuries ago. [Check Text 6(b) for examples.]
- In GA the season following summer is referred to as the *fall*, as used to be the case in British English where the term *autumn* is now used.
- In GA the word *mad* is frequently used to mean 'angry', a sense that was fairly common in British Early Modern English, but is less so now.

EXERCISE ✎

12.3 How valid are the comparisons made in the above paragraph for *all* of American English and *all* of British English? If you are familiar with British English, consider whether any of the supposedly American features do in fact appear in British English. If you are familiar with American English, consider whether any of the supposedly British features do in fact appear in American English.

There never have been any major linguistic differences between British and American English. Moreover, the last hundred years or so have seen increasing similarity between British and American English. This has partly been due to ever-improving communication systems, but also to the impact of American culture, notably through television and film.

EXERCISES ✎

12.4 Test your familiarity with near equivalent words in British and American English by filling the gaps.

British English	American English	American English	British English
trainers		candy	
vest		carryall	
waistcoat		cookie	
motorway		cot	
torch		diaper	
braces		drapes	
petrol		faucet	
shop assistant		public school	

12.5   All of the following words are currently used in British English. Which of them have come from American English? (Guess first, then check in a dictionary.)

> belittle, blizzard, blurb, cafeteria, cocktail (the drink), electrocute, jazz, radio, stooge, swamp

Other important varieties of English include those of Australia, Canada, Ireland, New Zealand and South Africa, where English is principally a native language, and also various countries in Africa, the subcontinent of India, the Caribbean and south-east Asia, where English is principally a second language. In each of these countries English has acquired its own distinctive characteristics and developed its own literature. Perhaps an indication that these literatures have come of age is the fact that the 1992 Nobel Prize for Literature was awarded to the Caribbean poet Derek Walcott.

Earlier in this book, we noted the settlement of Britain by the Anglo-Saxons, Scandinavians and French, and the linguistic consequences of bringing different languages into contact. Though such dramatic settlements have not been repeated, immigration is still an important factor in explaining the development of many varieties of English. For example, features of Irish English, such as the use of *yous* for plural *you*, can be heard in Liverpool. Indeed, this particular feature of Irish English can also be heard in Australia and many parts of the United States. All these places have experienced Irish immigration in the last 200 years.

EXERCISES ✎

12.6   The words below are fairly well known in most world Englishes. But in which variety of English did each of the words originate? Where possible, also try to identify which language supplied the word to English.

> aardvark, amok, apartheid, bangle, boomerang, bungalow, calypso, caribou, commando, cot, dungaree, guru, jodhpurs, juggernaut, jungle, kangaroo, kayak, kiwi, loot, parka, punch (the drink), pundit, pyjama, reggae, safari, shampoo, thug, veranda, voodoo, yoga, zebra

12.7   Guess the background of the speaker of Text 9(c), including where they come from. Draw up a list of features which strike you as distinctive. Now read the answer to this exercise.

It is sometimes claimed that English as an international language will succumb to the same fate as Latin. Around 2,000 years ago, Latin was used throughout western Europe, North Africa and Asia Minor (i.e. including the area covered by today's Turkey). Today, Latin is a dead language, and its descendants – such as Italian, French and Spanish – are separate languages. Do you think this prophecy is likely to be fulfilled? Will English become a group of English languages which are not mutually comprehensible?

If you are part of a group, set up a debate: half argue in support of the prophecy, and half against it. (*Hint:* It may help to consider spoken and written forms of language separately.)

DISCUSSION POINT

SUMMARY

- The last few centuries have seen the rapid expansion of English in terms of where it is found in the world, the number of uses to which it is put and the number of users.
- The most important national varieties are British English and American English, owing to imperial and economic power.
- In the beginning – the early seventeenth century – American English and British English grew apart, but more recently, with improved communications and the popularity of American culture, they are growing closer together.
- American English does contain a few features which are archaic from the point of view of British English. However, how many archaic features can be identified rather depends on which particular varieties of British and American English are considered.
- Distinctive varieties of English have developed across the globe.
- Immigration is still an important factor in the development of many varieties of English.

David Crystal covers world Englishes in some detail in his *Encyclopedia of the English Language* (Cambridge: Cambridge University Press, 1995). On pp. 92–105 he describes the establishment of varieties of English outside Britain; on pp. 106–15 he discusses English as a world language and considers the future of English; and on pp. 306–17 he focuses on American English, and on pp. 336–63 other varieties of English. A highly relevant and easy-to-read commentary can also be found in R. McCrum, W. Cran and R. MacNeil's *The Story of English* (London: Faber & Faber/BBC, 1992), Chapters 6–9. If you are interested in how varieties of language develop as a result of contact between languages, try Mark Sebba's *Contact Languages: Pidgins and Creoles* (London: Macmillan, 1997), where Chapters 7 and 9 consider varieties touched on in Exercise 12.7.

FOLLOW-UP READING

APPENDIX I: READING AN *OED* ENTRY

Below is the first part of the *OED* entry for the word *experience*. Note that guidance on abbreviations can be found at the beginning of the dictionary.

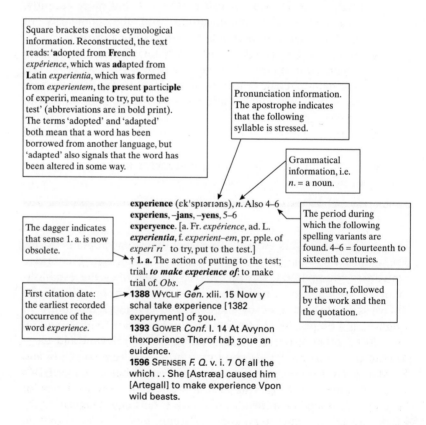

Square brackets enclose etymological information. Reconstructed, the text reads: 'adopted from **F**rench *expérience*, which was **ad**apted from **L**atin *experientia*, which was **f**ormed from *experientem*, the **pr**esent **participle** of experiri, meaning to try, put to the test' (abbreviations are in bold print). The terms 'adopted' and 'adapted' both mean that a word has been borrowed from another language, but 'adapted' also signals that the word has been altered in some way.

Pronunciation information. The apostrophe indicates that the following syllable is stressed.

Grammatical information, i.e. *n.* = a noun.

The dagger indicates that sense 1. a. is now obsolete.

The period during which the following spelling variants are found. 4–6 = fourteenth to sixteenth centuries.

First citation date: the earliest recorded occurrence of the word *experience*.

The author, followed by the work and then the quotation.

experience (ɛk'spɪərɪəns), *n.* Also 4–6 **experiens, –jans, –yens,** 5–6 **experyence.** [a. Fr. *expérience*, ad. L. *experientia*, f. *experient–em*, pr. pple. of *experiˉriˉ* to try, put to the test.]
† **1. a.** The action of putting to the test; trial. *to make experience of*: to make trial of. *Obs.*
1388 WYCLIF *Gen.* xlii. 15 Now y schal take experience [1382 experyment] of ʒou.
1393 GOWER *Conf.* I. 14 At Avynon thexperience Therof haþ ʒoue an euidence.
1596 SPENSER *F. Q.* v. i. 7 Of all the which . . She [Astræa] caused him [Artegall] to make experience Vpon wild beasts.

80

APPENDIX II: PHONETIC TRANSCRIPTION

The set of symbols used to represent speech sounds in this book is that used by David Crystal in his *Encyclopedia of the English Language* (Cambridge: Cambridge University Press, 1995) 237 and 242. Crystal follows the system devised by the British phonetician A.C. Gimson in *An Introduction to the Pronunciation of English* (1st edn, London: Edward Arnold, 1962). The reasons why this book uses this system are twofold: (a) Crystal's book is a key source of readings in this book and thus it makes sense to be consistent with it; and (b) Gimson's system has been particularly influential and is known throughout the world. Readers from the United States may wish to note that Crystal (p. 237) shows how Gimson's system relates to that used in Fromkin and Rodman's *An Introduction to Language* (5th edn, New York: Holt, Rinehart & Winston, 1992), a widely used textbook in the United States. To illustrate these symbols, what accent should be used? Different speakers may pronounce words differently, so it is difficult to suggest a word which illustrates a particular speech sound. In fact, an individual speaker may lack sounds that other speakers have or, conversely, may have sounds that other people don't have. In common with the books noted above, and indeed many other textbooks and dictionaries, I use *Received Pronunciation* (*RP*). This well-known British accent is sometimes referred to as the Queen's English, BBC English or simply 'talking posh', and is associated with educated speakers living in the south-east of England. (We look at the development of RP in **Unit 11**.) Beneath the symbols given below, I have suggested a few of the variations speakers of other accents might have. Some of these variations are considered in **Unit 10**. Moreover, it is well worth referring to Crystal's fuller description of regional variants (pp. 240–1 and 244–5). The illustrative words I use are almost all taken from Crystal (pp. 237 and 242).

The symbols below are divided into consonants and vowels. The symbol **ː** is used to signal a long vowel. The convention in this book for indicating a speech sound symbol, as opposed to spelling, is to place the symbol between square brackets, e.g. [v] for the last sound in *of*.

Consonants

p	*pie, up*	f	*fee, off*	h	*he*
b	*by, ebb*	v	*view, of*	m	*me, am*
t	*tie, at*	θ	*thigh, oath*	n	*no, in*
d	*die, odd*	ð	*they, booth*	ŋ	*hang*
k	*coo, ache*	s	*so, us*	l	*lie, eel*
g	*go, egg*	z	*zoo, ooze*	r	*row, ear* (not RP)
tʃ	*chew, each*	ʃ	*shoe, ash*	w	*way*
dʒ	*jaw, edge*	ʒ	*genre, rouge*	j	*you*

Glottal stop

Variations: Instead of [t], many speakers, typically Cockney and urban speakers, will use a GLOTTAL STOP [ʔ]. For example, in words like '*bottle*' the '*t*' sound is replaced by a sound which is made by closing the vocal cords and does not involve the tip of the tongue. Writers sometimes *suggest* glottal stops with apostrophes (e.g. *be'er* for *better*). In the United States, speakers often replace [t] between vowels (e.g. in words like *butter*) with a sound which is closer to [d].

Vowels

iː	*sea, feet, me, field*	ɜː	*bird, her, turn, learn*
ɪ	*him, big, village, women*	ə	*the, oppose, sofa, about*
e	*get, fetch, head, Thames*	eɪ	*ape, waist, they, say*
æ	*sat, hand, ban, plait*	aɪ	*time, cry, die, high*
ʌ	*sun, son, blood, does*	ɔɪ	*boy, toy, noise, voice*
ɑː	*calm, are, father, car*	əʊ	*so, road, toe, know*
ɒ	*dog, lock, swan, cough*	aʊ	*out, how, house, found*
ɔː	*all, saw, cord, more*	ɪə	*deer, here, fierce, near*
ʊ	*put, wolf, good, look*	eə	*care, air, bare, bear*
uː	*soon, do, soup, shoe*	ʊə	*poor, sure, tour, lure*

Variations: Speakers in the north of England do not have the vowel [ʌ], but instead use [ʊ]. They are also likely to produce [æ] further back in the mouth towards [ɑː]. Scottish and Irish accents do not have long [ɑː], but may use a short [ɑ] or a vowel towards [æ]. For many speakers of American English, the vowels [ɒ] and [ɔː] may not be distinguished (speakers from the south-west of the United States are likely to use [ɑ] for both). For speakers who pronounce *r* when it follows a vowel, the vowels which precede *r* are likely to be shorter. For example, the RP pronunciations of *car*, *bird*, *deer*, *care* and *poor* are [kɑː], [bɜːd], [dɪə], [keə] and [pʊə], but for many speakers from the United States they may be closer to [kɑr], [bərd], [dɪr], [ker] and [pʊr].

APPENDIX III: A 'MINI-CORPUS' OF TEXTS

TEXT 1

This text comes from the prologue of the *Anglo-Saxon Chronicle*, a yearly history of important events, written in the ninth century. A word-for-word translation is given in the line below. In the original text, you will come across the Runic character 'wynn', which was written somewhat like a *p*, except that the bottom of the descending stroke would flow back. This character was not familiar to Norman scribes, who replaced it in the eleventh century by *w*.

> Brittene igland is ehta hund   mila lang·
> Britain   island is eight hundred miles long
>
> 7 twa hund   brad· 7 her   sind on þis
> & two hundred broad & here are in this
>
> iglande fif geþeode· englisc· 7 brit
> island five languages English & Brit-
>
> tisc· 7 wilsc· 7 scyttisc· 7 pyhtisc· 7
> tish & Welsh & Scottish & Pictish &
>
> bocleden·   Erest peron bugend   þises
> book-Latin first were inhabitants of this
>
> landes brittes·
> land   Britons

TEXT 2

This text is from John of Trevisa's translation of the *Polychronicon*, a history of the world written in Latin by Ralph Higden. The translation was finished in 1387, and represents the southern dialect, or, more specifically, that of Gloucestershire. Here Trevisa writes about the accents of England. You will come across the versatile character 3 (called 'yogh'), which is frequent in many Middle English texts. Today, it would typically be replaced by *y*, *g* or *gh*, and sometimes *w* or *s*. The following punctuation is not original.

[. . .] for men of þe est wiþ men of þe west, as hyt [= *it*] were undur þe same party of hevene, acordeþ more in sounyng of speche [i.e. in pronunciation] þan men of þe norþ wiþ men of þe souþ. þerfore hyt ys þat Mercii [= *the Mercians*], þat buþ [= *are*] men of myddel Engelond, as hyt were parteners of þe endes, understondeþ betre þe syde longages, norþeron and souþeron, þan norþeron and souþeron understondeþ eyþer oþer. Al þe longage of þe Norþhumbres, and specialych at ʒork, ys so scharp, slyttyng [= *cutting*] and frotyng [= *grating*] and unschape, þat we souþeron men may þat longage unneþe [= *hardly*] understonde. Y trowe [= *believe*] þat þat ys bycause þat a [= *they*] buþ nyʒ [= *near*] to strange men and aliens [= *foreigners*] þat spekeþ strangelych, and also bycause þat þe kynges of Engelond woneþ [= *dwell*] fer fram þat contray; for a buþ more yturned [= *turned*] to þe souþ contray, and ʒef [= *if*] a goþ to þe norþ contray a goþ wiþ gret help and strengthe.

TEXT 3

This text is part of William Caxton's prologue to the *Eneydos* (his translation of the French version of the Latin poem *The Aeneid* by Virgil), printed in 1490. He recounts a story about some merchants who tried to ask for eggs in Kent.

And certaynly our langage now vsed varyeth ferre from that. whiche was vsed and spoken whan I was borne / For we englysshe men / ben borne vnder the domynacyon of the mone. whiche is neuer stedfaste / but euer wauerynge / wexynge one season / and waneth & dyscreaseth another season / And that comyn englysshe that is spoken in one shyre varyeth from a nother. In so moche that in my dayes happened that certayn marchauntes were in a shippe in tamyse [= *the river Thames*] for to haue sayled ouer the see into ʒelande [= *Holland*] and for lacke of wynde thei taryed atte forlond. [= *Foreland*] and wente to lande for to refreshe them And one of theym named sheffelde a mercer cam in to an hows and axed for mete. and specyally he axyd after eggys And the good wyf answerde. that she coude speke no frenshe. but wold haue hadde egges / and she vnderstode hym not / And thenne at laste a nother sayd that he wolde haue eyren / then the good wyf sayd that she vnderstod hym wel / Loo what sholde a man in thyse dayes now wryte. egges or eyren / certaynly it is harde to playse euery man / by cause of dyuersite & chaunge of langage.

This text is a letter written in 1497. The Celys were London **TEXT 4**
merchants. Here Richard Cely writes 'in haste' to his family to tell
them of a battle between France and Burgundy.

> I grete you wyll I late [= *let*] you wit [= *know*] of seche
> tydyng as I here Thomas blehom hatth a letter from caleys
> [= *Calais*] the weche ys of a batell done on sater^{day} last
> paste be syde trywyn [= *Tirwin*] be [= *by*] the dwke of
> borgan & the frynche kyng the weche batell be gane on
> sater day at iiij [= *4*] of the cloke at after non and laste
> tyll nyght & meche blode schede of bothe pertys and
> the dwke of borgan hathe the fylde and the worschepe
> the dwke of borgan hathe gette meche ordenons [=
> *ordnance*] of frenche kyngys and hathe slayne v or vj ml
> [= *5 or 6 thousand*] frensche men wryte on thorys day
> noe in haste
>
> p Rc cely [= *(per) by Richard Cely*]

The first two extracts below come from Shakespeare's *Richard III*.   **TEXT 5**
In extract (a) Richard of Gloucester and his supporter, the Duke of
Buckingham, are stage-managing an appearance before the people,
in which Richard poses as a saintly religious figure. In extract (b)
Richard is now king. Buckingham attempts to collect his reward,
promised for loyal support. Extract (c) comes from *All's Well That
Ends Well*. Here the Countess is attempting to establish whether
Helena loves her son. The spelling and punctuation are not original
in any extract.

(a)

GLOU.: [. . .] what is your Grace's pleasure?
BUCK.: Even that, I hope, which pleaseth God above,
And all good men of this ungovern'd isle.
GLOU.: I do suspect I have done some offence
That seems disgracious in the city's eye,
And that you come to reprehend my ignorance.
BUCK.: You have, my lord. Would it might please your
Grace,
On our entreaties, to amend your fault!
GLOU.: Else wherefore breathe I in a Christian land?
BUCK.: Know then, it is your fault that you resign
The supreme seat, the throne majestical [. . .]
(III.vii.108–18)

(b)

Buck.:	I am thus bold to put your Grace in mind
	Of what you promis'd me.
K. Rich.:	Well, but what's o'clock?
Buck.:	Upon the stroke of ten.
K. Rich.:	Well, let it strike.
Buck.:	Why let it strike?
K. Rich.:	Because that like a Jack thou keep'st the stroke
	Betwixt thy begging and my meditation.
	I am not in the giving vein to-day.
Buck.:	May it please you to resolve me in my suit.
K. Rich.:	Thou troublest me; I am not in the vein.

(IV.ii.114–22)

(c)

Count.:	Do you love my son?
Hel.:	Your pardon, noble mistress.
Count.:	Love you my son?
Hel.:	Do not you love him, madam?
Count.:	Go not about; my love hath in't a bond
	Whereof the world takes note. Come, come, disclose
	The state of your affection [. . .]

(I.iii.177–81)

TEXT 6   These extracts are from the Authorised Version of the Bible, which was published in 1611. Extract (a) is from the New Testament, Luke 6: 27–32; extract (b) is from the Old Testament, Ezekiel 28: 1–4.

(a)

But I say vnto you which heare, Love your enemies, doe good to them which hate you,

Bless them that curse you, & pray for them which despite-fully vse you.

And vnto him that smiteth thee on the *one* cheeke offer also the other: and him that taketh away thy cloke, forbid not to take thy coat also.

Give to euery man that asketh of thee, and of him that taketh away thy goods, aske them not againe.

And as yee would that men should doe to you, doe yee also to them likewise.

For if yee love them which loue you, what thanke haue ye? for sinners also loue those that loue them.

(b)

The word of the LORD came againe vnto me, saying,

Sonne of man, say vnto the prince of Tyrus, Thus saith the Lord GOD; Because thine heart is lifted vp, and thou hast said, I *am* a God, I sit *in* the seate of God, in the middest of the seas; yet thou *art* a man, and not God, though thou set thine heart as the heart of God.

Behold, thou *art* wiser than Daniel: there is no secret that they can hide from thee.

With thy wisdome and with thine vnderstanding thou hast gotten thee riches, and hast gotten gold and siluer into thy treasures.

This text is from John Milton's *Areopagitica*, published in 1644.   **TEXT 7**

I deny not, but that it is of greatest concernment in the Church and Commonwealth, to have a vigilant eye how Bookes demeane themselves as well as men; and thereafter to confine, imprison, and do sharpest justice on them as malefactors: For Books are not absolutely dead things, but doe contain a potencie of life in them to be as active as that soule was whose progeny they are; nay they do preserve as in a violl the purest efficacie and extraction of that living intellect that bred them. I know they are as lively, and as vigorously productive, as those fabulous Dragons teeth; and being sown up and down, may chance to spring up armed men. And yet on the other hand unlesse warinesse be us'd, as good almost kill a Man as kill a good Book; who kills a Man kills a reasonable creature, Gods Image; but hee who destroyes a good Booke, kills reason it selfe, kills the Image of God, as it were in the eye.

TEXT 8

This text is from Robert Lowth's *English Grammar* (1762), one of the most influential grammar books ever published. Here he comments on the fact that Samuel Johnson had given rather short shrift to the discussion of English syntax. The italics appear in the original.

> *The last*
> English *Grammar that hath been*
> *presented to the public, and by the*
> *Person best qualified to have given*
> *us a perfect one, comprises the whole*
> *Syntax in ten lines. The reason,*
> *which he assigns for being so very*
> *concise in this part, is, "because*
> *"our Language has so little in-*
> *"flection, that its Construction*
> *"neither requires nor admits many*
> *"rules." In truth, the easier*
> *any subject is in its own nature, the*
> *harder it is to make it more easy by*
> *explanation; and nothing is com-*
> *monly more unnecessary, and at the*
> *same time more difficult, than to*
> *give a Demonstration in form of a*
> *proposition almost self-evident.*

TEXT 9

These texts represent different varieties of today's English. Text (a) is an insurance condition that appears on the back of Comet Superstore receipts. It is supposedly legally binding. Text (b) is the first part of a text that accompanies an advertisement for a child's drink. Information about the speaker of (c) is given in the answer to exercise 12.7. The spelling of this text has been altered to convey something of the pronunciation. The symbol % represents a glottal stop. $ represents an *l* pronounced more like [w].

(a)

All of the express terms, conditions and exceptions applicable to the insurance of the product are set out in the Certificate. The scope and extent of the insurance cannot be extended without the express written authority of the Insurer.

(b)

Who understands I need almost as much iron as Daddy?
 It may surprise you to learn that from the age of 6 months, a baby needs 90% as much iron as a 30 year old man. However, cow's milk is too low in iron and vitamins A & D to be a main drink for a growing baby.

(c)

One day me met a witch [...] me saw her dere, me sit down an she tell me all the story alrigh%? One story was about the ghost she see – this is the story whe she tell me wha% she see, alright. She, one day she te$ me dat she saw a ghost – or somefing like a ghost, a person who come in the house – she te$ me she pick up a brick and break i bones – de ting run like she no know what.

APPENDIX IV:
SOME ANSWERS

UNIT 1
The birth of
English

1.1 Placenames with a Celtic link tend to survive in areas which did not see settlement by the Germanic tribes – the Anglo-Saxons. Thus, such placenames dominate areas of Scotland to the north of Edinburgh and areas in the west of Britain, particularly Ireland, Wales and Cornwall.

1.4

(a) You probably found that surprisingly few placenames are transferred British placenames. Many placenames that look like transferred British placenames turn out to be biographic – the names of British aristocrats. Aboriginal placenames make up a substantial proportion of Australian placenames. (This proportion does not in fact reflect the rather small impact of Aboriginal languages on Australian English.)

(b) You probably discovered that British influence was highest for eastern states, French for southern states and Spanish for the western states. This, of course, reflects the spheres of influence of those three colonial powers.

UNIT 2
Investigating
change in
English

2.1

Writing: Unfamiliar letters include þ (later replaced by *th*, as in *this*) and 7 (which is similar to our ampersand symbol &). Many words have different spellings from today. Clearly, our *sh* used to be written *sc* (e.g. *englisc, brittisc, wilsc*). The main punctuation mark here is the 'punctus' [·], which we would think of as a full-stop; note, however, that it is positioned in the middle of the line and that it appears where we would not expect it. Capitals are rarely used and are notably absent from proper nouns (e.g. *englisc, brittisc, wilsc*).

Structure: Note that there were many other ways in which one could make a plural noun apart from adding a 's'. Look at the equivalent words for 'miles', 'languages' and 'inhabitants': they are all plurals, but none are marked with an 's'. In translating Old English one often has to supply extra prepositions, such as *of*. The order of words in the last 'sentence' is strange from today's point of view, particularly with regard to the position of the verb 'were'.

Words: Some words are not used today (e.g. *geþeode*, *bugend*). There is even a different word for 'are'.

Meaning: The words *brittisc* and *brittes* do not have today's meaning. They refer to the Celtic tribes that used to inhabit Britain. In fact, *brittisc* and *wilsc* were one and the same language – Brito-Welsh – and this explains why the writer says that there are five languages and then appears to list six.

2.4 Typically, the older pronunciation stresses the first syllable, and the newer pronunciation the second syllable. This development has not been followed in the United States, where the first syllable is stressed.

3.1 These, of course, are some of the now infamous silent consonants of English spelling. Medial *w*, medial *l*, and initial *w*, *g* and *k* were almost certainly once pronounced.

UNIT 3
Spellings and speech sounds

3.3 The letter *v* is only used at the beginning of a word, and this convention is used by many other writers. In Text 3, *i* and *y* do seem fairly interchangeable. We would need to consider a larger sample of text to come to any firm conclusions, but given the text that we have, it seems to be the case that *i* is usually used at the beginning of a word.

3.4 You might want to consider words such as *ghost* and *ghoul*, and *graffiti* and *anti*.

3.5
(a)   The addition of the final -*e* (after a single consonant) signals a preceding long vowel. A few counter-examples, such as *some* and *give*, can be found.

(b)   The doubled consonant signals a preceding short vowel. Counter-examples, such as *fall*, are rare.

3.6
(a)   Potential problems include silent letters and the fact that schwa [ə] has no corresponding letter, but can be represented in a number of different ways in English.

(b)   These words have troublesome spellings, because they have been borrowed from other languages – Latin, French and Greek – and reflect the spelling conventions of those languages.

UNIT 4
Borrowing words

4.2

(a)   The large proportion of French-derived vocabulary in Text 9(a) contributes to its legal stylistic flavour. The vocabulary of Text 9(b) is overwhelmingly Germanic, making it a very accessible text with a conversational flavour – something that is clearly in the advertiser's interests. There are just three exceptions: *surprise* (a fifteenth century loan from Old French), *vitamins* (a twentieth century loan from Latin) and % (= *per cent*) (a sixteenth century loan from Latin, probably via Italian).

(b)   Text 3 contains largely Germanic vocabulary, except for some words derived from French. Text 7 also includes a number of words borrowed from Latin. This can be partly explained by noting that Text 3 was written before the dramatic Renaissance influx of Latin vocabulary. It also reflects the fact that Milton was writing a scholarly text for a highly educated audience.

4.4   Keith Waterhouse's advice seems to be of little value. Think of contexts where you would use one of a pair and then try swapping it with the other. You'll find a number of differences. Taking the pair *penniless* and *penurious* as an example, you'll find: *penniless* is only used to describe humans, whereas *penurious* never is; *penurious* has a slightly more negative tinge to its meaning than *penniless*, which tends simply to describe a state; *penurious* only ever occurs before the noun to which it refers, whereas *penniless* can occur both before or after; and *penurious* is a more formal word than *penniless*.

UNIT 5
New words from old

5.1   *anti-dis-establish-ment-arian-ism.*

UNIT 6
Changing meanings

6.1

(a) *Woman* suggests physical aspects; *lady* suggests social aspects.
(b) *Pretty* suggests delicate and dainty features; *handsome* suggests large and regular features.
(c) The data sets vary on a scale from formal to informal. *Cast* suggests religious language, *throw* is neutral and *chuck* slang. *Steed* sounds poetic, *horse* is neutral and *nag* slang.

6.2   Examples (b), (c), (e), (g), and (h) contain metaphors.

6.3   The main metaphor is disease. It is used because a more technical description would not be understood by many people.

7.2 A possible punctuated version would be:

> 'O king', they cried, 'there is no one so mighty as you!'
> 'Do all things obey me?' he asked. 'There is nothing that
> dares to disobey you, O king!' they cried. 'Will the sea
> obey me?' he asked. 'Command it, O king, and it will
> obey', said one. 'Sea', cried Canute, 'I command you to
> come no further!'

People from the United States are likely to use double quotation marks.

7.3 The main punctuation mark is the 'punctus' [·] and capitals are also used. The punctus is quite versatile: it appears where we would use a comma (e.g. in the list of languages), where we would use a full-stop (e.g. after *bocleden*), and where we would use nothing at all (e.g. after *lang*). In this text sample, the punctus is typically used to separate information in list constructions. Note that it almost always occurs before 7, the abbreviated 'and'. Capitals are used at the beginning of the text, and to introduce a development of topic, but not for proper nouns (e.g. the names of languages). Thus, broadly speaking, punctuation seems to be attempting to display the information structure of the text, and is thus partly grammatical and partly rhetorical. This would be consistent with the fact that the text is a written record. Of course, more text would be needed to confirm these ideas, and one certainly cannot assume that they will hold good for other texts of the period.

7.5 Caxton's punctuation is well known for being rather idiosyncratic and inconsistent. He uses a form of punctuation – the virgule (/) – that was to die out within a century of his writing. The virgule is usually used where we might put a full-stop or a comma ('For we englysshe men / ben borne [...]' is a clear exception). Sometimes the punctus is used at grammatical boundaries which would receive no punctuation today. For example, in 'the good wyf answerde. that she coude speke no frenshe' the conjunction 'that' is introducing the separate clause (or simple sentence) 'she coude speke no frenshe'. But, at other times, the punctus is used for no obvious reason: for example, in 'thei taryed atte forland. and wente to lande' the punctuation mark unhelpfully cuts off the second verb 'wente' from its subject 'thei'. (You will find a full description of the term 'subject' in **Unit 8**.) Capitals are not used for proper nouns. They appear after the punctus, the virgule and after nothing at all. One might argue that in general Caxton is not worried about the kind of punctuation mark he uses, but is simply trying to break up his text, perhaps to make it easier to read out.

7.6 Text 4 is striking for its almost total absence of punctuation, except for the odd capital letter. The use of conjunctions, such as *and*, helps us to cope with interpreting the text.

7.7   You should find that about two-thirds of all punctuation marks precede a conjunction. This concurrence suggests that punctuation is largely determined by the sense relationships between parts of the text.

7.8   The capitalisation in Texts 7 and 8 is not untypical of its period. Capitals appear at the beginning of sentences and of proper nouns, and in other places too. Like in modern German, many nouns begin with capitals, but not all. Usually nouns which are considered particularly important carry a capital.

UNIT 8
Grammar I:
nouns

8.2

(a)

    (1) He (subject) sees him (object)

    (2) Him (object) he (subject) sees

    (3) He (subject) sees his (possessor) face

(b)   In Text 6, the usage of second-person pronouns is grammatical (e.g. *ye* is only used as a plural subjective form, *you* as a plural objective form), even though this was not generally the case at the time. But note that we are looking at biblical language, which by its very nature is archaic. The Authorised Version reflects the language of at least fifty years before its publication date of 1611. In contrast, the usage of second-person pronouns in Texts 5(a) and (b) is governed by social factors. Clearly, in 5(a) Richard does not use *thou* forms to Buckingham, since it is in his interest to appear humble. Note that *your* collocates with the deferential term of address *Grace*. In 5(b) we see an asymmetric usage of pronouns. Buckingham, as before, uses polite *you* forms, but Richard has switched to *thou* forms. Before this extract, Buckingham has been quite persistent in trying to claim what he has been promised. In this extract, Richard's patience snaps and he viciously puts Buckingham down. Note that *thy* collocates with Richard's description of Buckingham's conversational behaviour as *begging*.

8.6   You should find a clear trend whereby the *s*–genitive is used for animate nouns, particularly human nouns.

UNIT 9
Grammar II:
verbs

9.1

- *I walk the dog*: no inflection = the base or root form.
- *She walks the dog*: base form + *s* = the third person singular.
- *She walked the dog*: base form + *ed* = the simple past, as in this example. For many verbs the *+ed* inflection is also used to form the past participle. What is the past participle? Typically, the past participle follows the verbs *have* or *be*,

as in (1) *Helen has walked the dog* or (2) *The dog is being walked by Helen*. Note that for some verbs the simple past and the past participle can have different forms, e.g. *She rode into town* vs. *She has ridden into town*.

- *She is walking the dog*: base form + *ing* = the present participle. In this example, the present participle signals that the action has not been completed, but is on-going.

9.2 The *-eth* inflection was archaic at this time. This explains why it is found exclusively in Text 6 (i.e. *-s* does not appear): biblical language tends to be archaic.

9.3 Some examples: *drunken sailor, grief stricken, molten lead, shrunken head*.

10.3

(a) The pronunciation [uː] can still be heard in Northumberland and Scotland.
(b) *Thou* forms can still be heard in some northern dialects, particularly Yorkshire.
(c) Post-vocalic *r* can be heard in south-west England, parts of Lancashire, Scotland and Ireland. (Its pronunciation may have implications for the preceding vowel sound. See Appendix II.)
(d) The sound [ʌ] is not used in the north and Midlands of England. Instead, [ʊ] is generally used.
(e) The change to [ɑː] has not taken place in the north and Midlands of England.

10.4 These areas are all sparsely populated, relative to the south-east of England. This could explain why language change has been slower here. Contact with other people is a cause of language change.

**UNIT 10
Dialects in
British English**

11.1

(a) It is the third person singular inflection '-s', as in *walks*.
(b) *are, die, leg, want, get, both, give, same, they, them, their*.

**UNIT 11
Standard-
isation**

11.2
(a) We have seen in this book that all living languages are in a constant state of change. They cannot be fixed.

(b)

1 This sentence breaks the rule that you should not end a sentence with a preposition (it ends with five!). The rule follows the conventions of Latin.
2 This sentence breaks the rule that you should not split an

infinitive, i.e. *to* should immediately precede its verb (e.g. *to go* and not *to boldly go*). The rule follows Latin, in which the infinitive was just one word and thus could not be split.

3   It was (and sometimes still is) argued that *among* refers to more than two people, and thus *between* should be used here. The rule reflects the wish of some scholars to fix certain meanings to certain words, in spite of the fact that this does not reflect what people actually do.

4   This sentence breaks the rule that you should not use a double negative, because two negatives make a positive. The rule appeals to mathematical logic. Of course, language is not a system of mathematical logic. People often use multiple negatives for a strategic purpose, such as emphasis. We have also seen in **Unit 9** that people in the past regularly formed negative statements using multiple negatives. Today, multiple negatives are socially stigmatised.

11.3   The factors may include the following: the fact that one variety has particular prestige and is widely understood; the existence of a means for the widespread dissemination of one particular variety; the fact that one variety is given a national focus; the codification of one variety; and the adoption of one variety by the education system.

11.4   The 'tyres' analogy is misleading in a number of ways. In particular, it disguises the negative side of standardisation. Standardisation means the eradication of variety – the disappearance of regional diversity. Many people see a large part of their identity as invested at a regional level.

11.5   The word *standard* is used by many linguists simply to refer to a variety of language which has been standardised, i.e. which has experienced the factors given above in the answer to exercise 11.3. In everyday language, however, it is most frequently used to mean a certain level of quality, often referring to standards of morality and behaviour. Thus, the notion of *standard language* is often seen as a kind of yardstick against which you can measure the 'quality' of people's language. Following on from this, the term *non-standard* (used by many linguists simply to refer to varieties of language, such as regional varieties, that are not part of the standard) is often taken to mean 'substandard'. It is on the basis of these misunderstandings that politicians can be frequently heard advocating the *standard* and condemning any educationalists who suggest accommodating *non-standard* varieties.

12.1

(a) Some examples of ENL countries: United States, United Kingdom, Ireland, Canada, Australia, New Zealand.

(b) Some examples of ESL countries: India, Singapore, Hong Kong, Malawi, Philippines, Zimbabwe.

(c) Some examples of EFL countries: Russia, Japan, Spain, China, France, Greece.

12.3

- It is not the case that all areas of Britain use [ɑː] in these words: it is not heard in the north and Midlands of England, in Scotland or in Ireland. Conversely, in the United States [ɑː] can be heard in eastern New England, particularly the area around Boston.

- Post-vocalic *r* is pronounced in some areas of Britain: in south-west England, parts of Lancashire, Scotland and Ireland. Conversely, in the United States it is not pronounced in eastern New England or the coastal areas of the southern states.

- The merger of the vowels [ɒ] and [ɔː] is true for the area of the United States starting in Pennsylvania, extending west in a strip through the Midland states, and then spreading out to include most of the west. But it is not true for other areas. Conversely, in the British Isles many Scottish and Northern Irish speakers do not distinguish between these two vowels.

- This seems to be generally true: *gotten* is not used in British English.

- It is true that the word *fall* is rarely used in British English. However, *autumn* is frequently used in many varieties of American English.

- Broadly speaking, this is accurate. However, there is some evidence that *mad* meaning 'angry' is increasing in British English, particularly amongst young people.

12.4

British English	American English	American English	British English
trainers	sneakers	candy	sweets
vest	undershirt	carryall	holdall
waistcoat	vest	cookie	biscuit (roughly)
motorway	expressway/ freeway	cot	camp bed
torch	flashlight	diaper	nappy
braces	suspenders	drapes	curtains
petrol	gas	faucet	tap
shop assistant	salesclerk	public school	state school

An important point to note (and one which is disguised by this exercise) is that many differences between British and American English are not a matter of simple translation, but of distribution and frequency (e.g. *diaper* also occurs in Britain, but not as frequently as *nappy*).

12.7   The speaker is a twelve-year-old white girl, born in London to British-born parents. Features of London English include the use of glottal stops and the pronunciation of *l* so that it sounds more like [w]. But there are other features which are not distinctive of London. These include [ð] and [θ], as in the first sound of *the thing*, pronounced as [d] and [t]; the use of *me* as a subject pronoun; the lack of past-tense marking in *tell*, *see*, *pick* and *run*; and the use of *no* to form the negative construction *she no know what*. These features are more strongly associated with speakers living in the Caribbean, specifically, in Jamaica. Why does this speaker have features of what some have broadly labelled 'Caribbean English'? Most of the speaker's friends are black British people, the descendants of immigrants from the West Indies. More generally, one might also note that reggae music has popularised Caribbean speech amongst non-Caribbean youth. If you had guessed that this speaker came from the United States or Canada, you are not completely wrong, since immigration from the West Indies has also taken place there. Moreover, in the United States so-called 'Black English Vernacular', used by many people of black African background, has some features in common with Caribbean English, such as the replacement of word-initial [ð] with [d] (e.g. 'dat' for 'that'). Both Caribbean English and Black English Vernacular owe their origins to the enslavement of west Africans between the late sixteenth century and the mid-nineteenth century.

APPENDIX V: GENERAL READING

A cutting-edge textbook
Graddol, D., Leith, D. and Swann, J., *English: History, Diversity and Change*, London: The Open University and Routledge, 1966. (Particularly Chapters 2–5.)

Some standard works on the history of the English language
Baugh, A. and Cable, T., (4th edn), *A History of the English Language*, London: Routledge, 1993.
Pyles, T. and Algeo, J., (4th edn), *The Origins and Development of the English Language*, Fort Worth, TX: Harcourt Brace Jovanovich, 1993.

A standard work on the social history of the English language
Leith, D., *A Social History of English*, London: Routledge, 1983.

Some shorter and more readable works covering the history of the English language
Burchfield, R., *The English Language*, Oxford: Oxford University Press, 1985.
Crystal, D., *The English Language*, Harmondsworth: Penguin, 1988.

A fun book on the history of the English language
Bryson, B., *Mother Tongue: the English Language*, Harmondsworth: Penguin, 1990.

Some annotated source books
Burnley, D., *The History of the English Language*, London: Longman, 1992.
Freeborn, D., *From Old English to Standard English*, London: Macmillan, 1992.
Burnley, D., *The History of the English Language*, Longman, 1992.

An activity-based book on general language change
Trask, R.L., *Language Change*, London: Routledge, 1994.

INDEX